Small Water Enterprises in Africa
1: Tanzania

Small Water Enterprises in Africa 1: Tanzania

A study of small water enterprises in Dar es Salaam

Linus Materu and Mwanakombo Mkanga
Series Editors: Cyrus Njiru and Mike Smith

Water, Engineering and Development Centre
Loughborough University
2006

Water, Engineering and Development Centre,
Loughborough University,
Leicestershire, LE11 3TU, UK

© WEDC, Loughborough University, 2006

ISBN 13 Paperback: 978 1 84380 094 1
ISBN Ebook: 9781788533515
Book DOI: http://dx.doi.org/10.3362/9781788533515

A catalogue record for this book is available from the British Library.

A reference copy of this publication is also available online at:
http://www.lboro.ac.uk/wedc/publications/sftup.htm

Materu, L. and Mkanga, M. (2006)
Small Water Enterprises in Africa 1: Tanzania
A study of small water enterprises in Dar es Salaam

WEDC (The Water, Engineering and Development Centre) at Loughborough University in the UK is one of the world's leading institutions concerned with education, training, research and consultancy for the planning, provision and management of physical infrastructure for development in low- and middleincome countries.

This edition is reprinted and distributed by Practical Action Publishing.
Since 1974, Practical Action Publishing has published and disseminated books and information in support of international development work throughout the world. Practical Action Publishing trades only in support of its parent charity objectives and any profits are covenanted back to Practical Action (Charity Reg. No. 247257, Group VAT Registration No. 880 9924 76).

This document is an output from a project funded by the UK
Department for International Development (DFID)
for the benefit of low-income countries.
The views expressed are not necessarily those of DFID.

Designed and produced at WEDC by Kay Davey
Front cover photo montage by Rod Shaw
Front cover photographs by Cyrus Njiru
Illustrations by Ken Chatterton

Acknowledgements

The editors wish to express gratitude to the in-country study team comprising Linus Materu (Consulting Water Engineer, EWAREMA Consult) and Mwanakombo Mkanga (Research Officer, WaterAid, Dar es Salaam). The editors are also grateful to staff from EWAREMA and WaterAid (Dar es Salaam) for their assistance and support to the study team.

The editors wish to thank members of the UK research team, comprising Mike Albu, Diana Mitlin and Gordon McGranahan, for their important role in the research project.

Contents

List of figures

List of tables

Acronyms

CWS	City Water Services Ltd
DAWASA	Dar es Salaam Water and Sewerage Authority
DAWASCO	Dar es Salaam Water and Sewerage Corporation
DFID	Department for International Development
EWURA	Energy and Water Utilities Regulatory Authority
GoT	Government of Tanzania
HBS	Household Budget Survey
IDPM	Institute for Development Policy and Management
ITDG	Practical Action
	(formerly the Intermediate Technology Development Group)
IIED	International Institute for Environment and Development
MoWLD	Ministry of Water and Livestock Development
NUWA	National Urban Water Authority
SWE	Small Water Enterprise
TCU	Ten Cell Units
UWSA	Urban Water and Sewerage Authorities
UWSA	Urban Water Supply Authorities
WDC	Ward Development Committee
WEDC	Water, Engineering and Development Centre, Loughborough University

Executive Summary

Background

Phase 1 of the 'Better Access to Water in Informal Urban Settlements through Support to Small Water Enterprises' project was undertaken to develop a contextual understanding and analyse the operating environment of small water enterprises (SWEs); to identify, assess and select interventions to improve the performance of SWEs for Phase 2; and to begin to build a more favourable environment for SWEs through contacts within the utilities and other relevant agencies.

The research was funded by the UK Department for International Development (DFID) and was carried out by the Water, Engineering and Development Centre (WEDC) at Loughborough University, UK. The local partner for this research was WaterAid, which is an international NGO active in the water sector, and with a presence in Tanzania, where it has an urban programme.

The study was carried out in the five sub-wards of Sandali Ward previously known as Temeke Mikoroshini, in the Temeke Municipality in the southern part of Dar es Salaam. The whole study area is an informal settlement occupied by low-income residents. The sub-wards are Mamboleo A, Mamboleo B, Sandal, Mwembeladu and Mpogo. They have a total population of 38,631 based on the 2002 Census.

Only small areas of the Mwembeladu and Sandali sub-wards have piped water from the utility responsible for water services in Dar es Salaam. The supply is unreliable and only available at certain times. This situation has created an environment conducive to street water vending and the reselling of utility water by neighbours with piped connections. The other sub-wards have no piped water. Most of the residents in all the wards rely mainly on private boreholes, community-managed boreholes, and municipal wells with handpumps. Some hand-dug wells are located in the riverbed of the nearby Yombo River.

National context

Tanzania's urban areas are expanding rapidly. The urban population is growing fast, exerting enormous pressure on the delivery of various services, including water supply services. About 70 per cent of the urban population live in unplanned or squatter areas. In addition to the generally poor housing, the areas are characterized by high population density and deficiencies in infrastructure services, including water. The people in these informal settlements collect water from kiosks or buy it from vendors at a price that is higher than that paid by people with house connections. People in urban areas have better drinking water supplies than the rural population.

In the current situation, the major issues and challenges facing the urban water sector include inadequate water supply both in quantity and quality; poor billing and revenue collection; lack of an enabling environment for private sector participation; and the belief that water is a god-given resource that should be free.

Dar es Salaam water situation

In general Tanzania has sufficient surface and groundwater resources to meet present needs, but it is unevenly distributed among the regions. Many urban water supply schemes, including Dar es Salaam, do not have adequate water storage, which makes them vulnerable to droughts.

From 1997 a total of 18 urban water systems managed by the then Ministry of Water (now Ministry of Water and Livestock Development, MoWLD) were handed over to independent and autonomous Urban Water and Sewerage Authorities (UWSA). The Dar es Salaam Water and Sewerage Authority (DAWASA) was also formed in 1997 by merging the former National Urban Water Authority (NUWA) with the Dar es Salaam Sewerage and Sanitation Department (DSSD) of the Dar es Salaam City Commission. Generally the service is still unreliable and the water delivered often unsafe for drinking. The situation is more critical in the informal urban settlements. Cholera outbreaks are common in many urban centres, including Dar es Salaam.

The informal settlements

The shortage of adequate housing in urban areas, especially in Dar es Salaam, prompted the newly independent government in 1961 to adopt various measures aimed at increasing the supply of adequate housing for city dwellers. By 1969 the government had realized that the strategy was grossly inappropriate, and in 1972 the government adopted a new policy towards informal settlement development. The main objective was to recognize the role and existence of informal housing areas and improve them. Houses in informal settlements are now accepted as part of the housing stock.

About 70 per cent of the population of Dar es Salaam live in unplanned settlements (MoLHSD, 2000). The unplanned settlements in Tanzania house both low-income and middle-income people. There are therefore unplanned areas with all the services such as water, solid waste collection and electricity. Different categories of housing include: unplanned/legal, unplanned/illegal, and planned legal settlements.

Low-income areas are essentially un-serviced by the water utility. Most people obtain their water from water vendors (who use pushcarts), privately owned shallow wells, and sales of utility water to neighbours and vendors.

The poor suffer most because often they have to buy water at prices that are many times higher than the official rate charged by the utility. The quality of the water delivered is also questionable.

Dar es Salaam has three districts/municipalities, namely Kinondoni, Ilala and Temeke. In each municipality there are a number of informal urban settlements.

The study was carried out in the five sub-wards of Sandali Ward in the Temeke Municipality of Dar es Salaam. The main sources of income for most households in the study area are petty trade (mainly in foodstuffs) and paid employment in either central and local government offices or public and private institutions and industries. There is no significant agricultural activity in the area. The people in the study area are affected by a number of diseases including malaria, diarrhoea, dysentery, cholera, HIV/AIDS, tuberculosis, and malnutrition among others.

The only surface water source in the area is the Yombo river which is heavily polluted by industrial wastewater discharges from industries located to the north of the settlement. Only small areas of the Mwembeladu and Sandali sub-wards have piped utility water. The supply has been unreliable for a long time and is only available during the night twice a week. Rainwater harvesting is practised but because of inadequate storage facilities not much water is stored.

Key findings

- *Coping strategies:* Water for different domestic uses is generally collected from different sources. For drinking and cooking purposes people prefer high quality water that tastes good, and they are willing to pay higher prices for such water. Households fetch water from the sources themselves in order to save money, and some have bought pushcarts to transport water for household use in order to save the money they would otherwise pay to vendors.

- **SWE livelihoods:** Street water vending provides employment mainly for young otherwise unemployed men aged between 18 and 30 years. There is competition between SWEs, and water vendors face competition from other suppliers on the basis of price. Owners of private boreholes, shallow wells and resellers of utility water deliberately reduce prices at the sources in order to encourage household customers to collect water directly from the sources. Young vendors, without dependants, are also able to reduce prices. Vendors previously rented pushcarts, but many now prefer to buy their own pushcarts to avoid rental charges. Vendors generally work independently, and do not co-operate with each other or share facilities.
- **Constraints to SWE activities:** Both SWEs and consumers have concerns about water quality. The SWEs agree that poor water quality is a constraint to their commercial business interests, whereas the consumers are suspicious about the quality of some of the vended water, and are concerned both for their health and well being and because they may be spending money from their meagre income on water of uncertain quality. The cost of water from vendors reflects the distance that pushcart vendors have to travel to fetch water from utility piped sources far away. Walking and pushing a cart over long distances in search of the high quality water demanded by customers and selling the water at a higher price is not a motivation to the vendors because the practice puts physical strain on their bodies. Vendors would prefer to have a piped water source nearby, and a local utility source would also be advantageous to the consumer in terms of quality and cost.
- **Consumers' perspectives:** Consumers were in agreement that the SWEs (street water vendors, private borehole owners, community-managed boreholes, utility kiosks managed by communities, neighbours with utility private water connection /yard tap) operating in the Sandali Ward were providing an indispensable service to the people living in the settlement and at the same time were creating employment for themselves. Consumers see SWEs as playing a valuable role in the provision of water supply services to un-served and/or under-served households, a role which the utilities and government have not yet managed to fulfil. Cost and water quality were important criteria for customers.
- **Utility perspectives:** Most utility stakeholders and officials support installing utility kiosks to deliver water to households and street water vendors at a controlled price. Installation of utility kiosks will provide opportunities for interaction/partnership between SWEs and utilities for mutual benefit and service to the consumers. In the short-term, even if the utility does not recognize SWEs, SWEs will continue to provide their services to bridge the supply gap left by the utilities in the informal settlements. Some utility staff consider that

provision of water by SWEs might not be desirable because it is difficult to control prices and water quality, especially for street water vendors.

Conclusions

The existing water supply infrastructure in the study area is unable to meet the ever-increasing demand for water. SWEs are respected and accepted in the local community because of their water supply services, and they therefore have a guaranteed market for their services, because of the inadequate utility water supply. The scarcity of utility water supply services is offering employment to water vendors and kiosk attendants in the settlements.

In the short-term, the focus of improvement measures will be on the quality of water from the private boreholes and other related factors, including price of water, and the mutual benefit of the communities, utilities and the borehole operators (SWEs). The revised National Water Policy also supports assessment and recognition of SWEs, who comprise the local informal private sector.

The problems of poor water quality and high prices charged by vendors could be alleviated by extending utility distribution pipelines to the unserved or inadequately served informal settlements and installing utility kiosks that will provide good quality water at affordable prices.

Way forward

The following factors/issues were raised by consumers, SWEs and utilities in the course of the study:

- Demand for utility piped water by consumers
- Reduced distance to source and reduced price
- Improved water quality
- Reliability of supply
- Health hazards on the part of vendors as a result of long distance travel pushing carts

A way forward is to address the above issues, through provision of kiosks within the study area, as kiosks are widely perceived to be the most appropriate method for providing water of good quality at controlled and affordable prices. Provision of kiosks, and monitoring how the kiosks are managed, should include:

- Extension of utility distribution pipe to the settlement to supply water through kiosk(s). It is also proposed to install a water storage tank at each kiosk, to help maintain regular supplies.

- Involvement of the community (households and community leaders) in the appropriate location of the pilot kiosk. This approach is meant to ensure that the community participates in the planning process for the intervention.
- Empowerment of SWEs (private borehole owners, community-managed boreholes, and pushcart water vendors) to operate the kiosks through contractual agreement with the utilities. This approach will create opportunities for partnerships between SWEs and the utilities.
- Use of NGOs in the involvement of communities in project planning, capacity building of SWEs, creation of awareness on environmental and health issues among SWEs, and promotion of public awareness of SWEs activities.

Chapter 1

Introduction

1.1   Background

This study 'Better Access to Water in Informal Urban Settlements through Support to Small Water Enterprises in Dar es Salaam' is part of a wider study on 'Better access to water in informal urban settlements through small water enterprises' funded by the UK Department for International Development (DFID). Other countries involved in the study are Ghana, Kenya, and Sudan.

1.2   Goal, purpose and outputs of the study

The project goal and purpose were spelled out in the terms of reference for the study:

- The **goal** of the study is *to raise the well being of the poor in informal urban settlements through cost-effective improved water supply services.*
- The **purpose** of the study is *to identify and test constraints, opportunities and strategies for enabling small-scale independent providers to deliver acceptable water service to poor urban consumers.*

1.3   Study focus, aims and objectives

The study focus, aims and objectives as specified in the terms of reference are described below.

Study focus

The focus of the study was provision of water in the unserved or inadequately served low-income urban settlements where conventional water supply is very limited. The research was required to build on the available knowledge of small-scale private sector providers of water referred to as Small Water Enterprises (SWEs), so as to develop practical methods of enabling them to play a more effective part in the provision of water, in partnership with water utilities. The research also investigated what market incentives exist for better water services, and how these can be realised.

Phase 1 of the research was required to summarize existing knowledge of SWEs in Dar es Salaam and further explore the experiences, attitudes and perceptions of consumers, providers and utilities. The research would also investigate existing market incentives for provision of better water services through SWEs and how these could be realized. Phase 2 of the study will develop pilot interventions that can benefit all stakeholder groups (consumers, utilities and SWEs) through sustainable working agreements between utilities and SWEs.

Study aims
The key aims of the study were defined in the terms of reference as follows:

(i)   To obtain a more in-depth understanding of the way in which water vending fits into the livelihood strategies of vendors.
(ii)   To develop a better understanding of how tariff structures and payment systems can enhance the financial viability of utilities and SWEs, while keeping water services affordable to consumers.
(iii)   To identify what kinds of support there could be for SWEs, and from whom.
(iv)   To explore how issues of water quality control could be addressed.
(v)   To test some of the recommendations that emerge from Phase 1 through pilot work in partnership with stakeholders during Phase 2.

1.4   Anticipated study outputs
The three principal outputs expected from this study are:

i)   A Country Status Report by the end of Phase 1, describing the water supply context in Tanzania and in Dar es Salaam based on information from utilities and from central and local government, NGOs and academics. The report should define opportunities to improve services provided by small water enterprises to poor consumers.
ii)   Documentation of action research piloting interventions by the end of Phase 2 to encourage constructive relations and collaboration between SWEs and utilities, support SWEs, and remove specific barriers to provision of water services by SWEs.
iii)   Targeted dissemination of the findings by the end of Phase 2, especially those relating to encouragement of good practice and business development.

1.5   The study team
The study team consisted of UK-based members and in-country researchers.

The UK-based team consisted of Mr Mike Smith – Project/Programme Manager, WEDC; Dr Cyrus Njiru – Research Manager/Principal Researcher, WEDC; Mr Mike Albu – Enterprise Development Specialist, ITDG; Dr Diana Mitlin – Social Development Specialist, IIED/IDPM; and Dr Gordon McGranahan – Development Economist, IIED.

The in-country research team consisted of Mr Linus W. Materu – Consulting Water Engineer from EWAREMA Consult; Mwanakombo Mkanga – Research Officer, WaterAid–Dar es Salaam; Ms Sophia Komba – Sociologist; Mrs Eda Gweba – Community Development Staff, Temeke Municipal Council; and Mr Mwita Maswa – Water Technician, WEPMO. Thanks also go to all from WaterAid's Dar es Salaam Office.

1.6   Structure of this report

The report has been structured to provide a systematic presentation of the key aspects concerning better access to water in informal urban settlements through support to small water enterprises.

Chapter 2 covers the national water supply context. It outlines the main water resources available, national institutional arrangements, and major changes under way.

Chapter 3 is on the water supply situation in Dar es Salaam and it covers the institutional reforms and administrative arrangements at different levels of local government; water supply coverage and demand; existing water supply sources and infrastructure; the legal and regulatory framework; and sub-sector maps that summarize information for Sandali district.

Chapter 4 gives an overview of current water policy issues – including private sector participation – focusing on issues influencing provision of water services to the poor in Dar es Salaam's informal settlements.

Chapter 5 is an overview of the types and significance of informal urban poor settlements in Dar es Salaam and their different forms of water services. The criteria used for selecting the research locations is provided in this chapter.

Chapter 6 focuses on the relationship between water and household poverty in the study area. It attempts to give an understanding of how inadequate access to water services impact on poverty and how poverty influences access to water services.

Chapter 7 gives an understanding of the structure, role and function of SWEs, the livelihoods of those who work in them, the forces that govern their working practices, their perceived constraints, and their hopes for a better working environment.

Chapter 8 provides consumer perspectives on water services provided by SWEs.

Chapter 9 provides information about the attitudes of government officials and water utility staff towards the goal of improving access to water in informal settlements, and the role that SWEs could play in achieving that goal.

Chapter 10 describes the conclusions of stakeholders concerning provision of feasible and effective ways of improving water supply to the informal settlements.

Recommendations for Phase 2 action research are given in Chapter 11.

The study methodology is described in Appendix 1.

Chapter 2

Water Supply – The National Context

2.1 Overview

Tanzania's urban areas are expanding rapidly. The urban population of 6 million people (World Bank Project Appraisal, 2003b) is growing at a rate of 4.2 per cent per annum, which is exerting enormous pressure on the delivery of various services, including water supply services. About 70 per cent of the urban population live in unplanned or squatter areas. In addition to the generally poor housing, the areas are characterized by high population density and deficiencies in infrastructure services, including water. The people in these informal settlements collect water from kiosks or buy it from vendors at a price that is higher than that paid by people with house connections. The existing water sources and water supply infrastructures are old and inadequate to meet the ever-increasing demand for water. Only about 73 per cent of the urban population have access to reliable (piped and protected sources) water supply services (MoWLD, 2002).

In the current situation, the major issues and challenges facing the urban water supply services sector include inadequate water supply both in quantity and quality; poor billing and revenue collection; lack of an enabling environment for private sector participation; and the belief that water is a god-given resource that should be free.

2.2 Drinking water

In general Tanzania has sufficient surface and groundwater resources to meet present needs, but it is unevenly distributed among the regions. Many urban water supply schemes, including Dar es Salaam, do not have adequate water storage, which makes them vulnerable to droughts.

The Household Budget Survey (HBS, 2002) of 2000/01 carried out in 20 regions of the Tanzanian mainland found that some 39 per cent of households use piped water, including private piped to inside the house, private piped to outside the house, piped to neighbour, and piped to community, and another 16 per cent use protected sources, including public and private wells and springs. Overall, 43 per cent of Tanzanian households use an unprotected source of drinking water, including unprotected public and private wells, springs, and surface water such as rivers and lakes.

People in urban areas have better drinking water supplies than the rural population. Some 53 per cent of rural households depend on an unprotected water supply, while 86 per cent of households in Dar es Salaam and 76 per cent in other urban areas have piped water of some kind (see Appendix 3, Table A3.1). The figure of 86 per cent for Dar es Salaam could be on the high side; the World Bank project appraisal report has assessed a lower figure of 75 per cent (see Section 3.4).

Access to water source
Trends in the 'distance to drinking water supplies' statistic are divergent, with a rise in households reporting a source within a kilometre but also an increase in those whose source is more than six kilometres away. Distance and time to water source give an indication of the burden of domestic water management felt by women and children in Tanzania and is an indication of time that could be spent on more productive and social activities.

The mean distance to drinking water in the dry season is given in Table A3.2 (Appendix 3).

According to HBS 2000/1, poor households are more likely to depend on unprotected sources and less likely to have piped water than households that are not poor.

Some 54 per cent of the poorest households depend on an unprotected source of drinking water, compared with 40 per cent of other households. The average distance to drinking water is also higher for the poorest, but the differences and the average distances are not large (see Appendix 3, Table A3.2).

2.3   Urban water supply and sewerage institutions
From 1997 a total of 18 urban water systems managed by the then Ministry of Water (now Ministry of Water and Livestock Development, MoWLD) were handed over to independent and autonomous Urban Water and Sewerage Authorities (UWSA). (They had operated as Urban Water and Sewerage Departments until declared Authorities under the Waterworks Ordinance.) Local Boards for UWSAs set consumer tariffs and UWSAs are expected to meet operation and maintenance costs. UWSAs have been divided into three categories (Gibb Eastern Africa, 2000). Category A authorities are completely independent with regard to all recurrent expenditure and are able to raise revenue to contribute towards an

annual development budget. Category B authorities retain their independence regarding recurrent operational expenditure but staff are still employed by government. Category C authorities retain their independence with regard to recurrent operational expenditures but government still covers all staff wages and power bills. The Dar es Salaam Water and Sewerage Authority (DAWASA) was also formed in 1997 by merging the former National Urban Water Authority (NUWA) with the Dar es Salaam Sewerage and Sanitation Department (DSSD) of the Dar es Salaam City Commission. Generally the service is still unreliable and the water delivered often unsafe for drinking. The situation is more critical in the informal urban settlements. Cholera outbreaks are common in many urban centres, including Dar es Salaam.

Chapter 3

Water Supply in Dar es Salaam

3.1 Brief history

Dar es Salaam is the national centre for industry, commerce, service and administration. It has a population of 2,497,940 based on the 2002 population census. It covers a total area of about 1,400 km^2 divided into three districts or municipalities: Kinondoni, Ilala and Temeke. Kinondoni has 27 administrative wards, Ilala 22, and Temeke 24. The annual population growth rate in 1998–2002 is 4.3 per cent (National Bureau of Statistics, 2002).

The first water supplies for Dar es Salaam were shallow wells and boreholes constructed within the city. As the city developed in the early 1950s the Kizinga River source and Mtoni water treatment works (7 km south of the city) were commissioned. In 1953 it was apparent that the Mtoni source was too small. A decision was made to use the Ruvu River, about 60 km west of the city, and implementation of the Upper Ruvu system started. The capacity of the system was increased in stages with the construction of the Lower Ruvu surface water scheme (about 20 km downstream of the Upper Ruvu intake works), commissioned in 1976.

More than 200 boreholes fitted with electric pumps and handpumps have been developed in the city since 1997, following a drought that affected many parts of the country, including the Ruvu river catchment area. These boreholes have helped to alleviate the shortages caused by either low flows in the Ruvu River during drought or occasional bursts of the major transmission mains which convey water from the Ruvu water supply schemes. The safe yield of the aquifer is not well known, however, and the quality of the water is questionable.

The water supply system was managed by the Dar es Salaam Water Supply Corporation up to 1984, when the National Urban Water Authority effectively took over. NUWA was established as a parastatal organization by an Act of Parliament (Number 7) of 1981.

The Dar es Salaam Water and Sewerage Authority (DAWASA) was established in 1997 by an Act of Parliament – Act Number 7 of 1981 – and amended by Act Number 8 of 1997 which merged the water supply operations of the defunct NUWA and the sewerage activities of the defunct Dar es Salaam Sewerage and Sanitation Department of the then Dar es Salaam City Commission.

Further amendments were made to the Act in 1999 to allow private sector participation in the delivery of water supply and sewerage services in Dar es Salaam, and again in 2000 to allow for the creation of a regulating authority.

In 2001, the government passed an act to create the Energy and Water Utilities Regulation Authority (EWURA).

All amendments were finally amalgamated into one main act, the Dar es Salaam Water and Sewerage Authority Act, 2001.

DAWASA's operational area includes the city of Dar es Salaam, Kibaha and Bagamoyo towns in the Coast Region, and rural settlements within a corridor on each side of the two transmission mains which convey treated water from the Upper and Lower Ruvu water treatment works to the city. It is estimated that about 150,000 people along the transmission mains are supplied with water.

3.2 Present institutional arrangements (prior to May 2005)

(Note that the research documented in this report was conducted prior to May 2005, when the Government of Tanzania terminated the lease contract with City Water. A new entity, DAWASCO, was then established, and DAWASCO inherited all management responsibilities from City Water. Since May 2005 responsibilities have been shared between DAWASA and DAWASCO. DAWASA is the Asset Holding Authority on behalf of the government, and DAWASCO uses DAWASA's infrastructure to provide water and sewerage services in the greater Dar-es-Salaam area.)

DAWASA institutional and contractual arrangements

The privatization of DAWASA started back in 1997. In February 2003, DAWASA signed a 10-year lease agreement with a locally incorporated private operator, City Water Services Ltd (CWS), to operate and maintain the water supply and sewerage assets and extend services to unserved areas. A Biwater/Gauff joint venture from the UK and Germany is the majority shareholder of the local company and manager for the operator. According to the contract actual operations commenced in August 2003.

Under this arrangement DAWASA, as the asset holding authority (AHA), is owned by the government and is responsible for the financing and implementation of water supply and sewerage facilities in the DAWASA designated service area. The government and DAWASA have entered into a 10-year development contract that specifies conditions under which the Capital Investment Programme is financed by the government and also specifies the responsibilities of DAWASA for contributing to implementation of the programme.

The operator will enter into a contract with customers and will collect bills from the customers.

EWURA will regulate the provision of water supply and sewerage services on behalf of the government and audit the private operator in relation to its licence. The authority is responsible for licensing both DAWASA and the operator, adjusting tariffs, and overall monitoring of the quality of performance in the water supply and sewerage service. It will employ technical, financial and economic consultants and auditors as necessary. Actual operations at EWURA have not yet started. However a coordinator for regulating services on behalf of the government is already in office.

It is too early now to comment on the efficacy of the reforms, present institutional arrangements, or utility performance.

The contractual arrangements are shown in Figure 3.1.

The city administrative setting
Three districts (which became municipalities at the end of 1999), 73 wards of the city of Dar es Salaam, and their sub-wards, represent the main levels of city government.

For administrative purposes, the wards are comprised of a number of sub-ward areas, which are called *mtaa* (meaning 'street', plural 'mitaa' in Kiswahili). The ward executive officer and the sub-ward or *Mtaa* leader are the government or city representatives in their local area. The ward executive officers are appointed and employed by the municipal authority, while the *mtaa* leaders are elected by the residents in their area and work on a voluntary basis. *Mtaa* leaders play important roles in mobilizing residents to pay local taxes, maintaining law and order, resolving disputes, and above all in spearheading community development in their areas.

The size of a *mtaa* area varies according to the geographical size of the ward and its population distribution.

The *mtaa* areas are divided into 'Ten Cell Units' (TCUs). They are the smallest political and administrative units put in place during the single-party era in

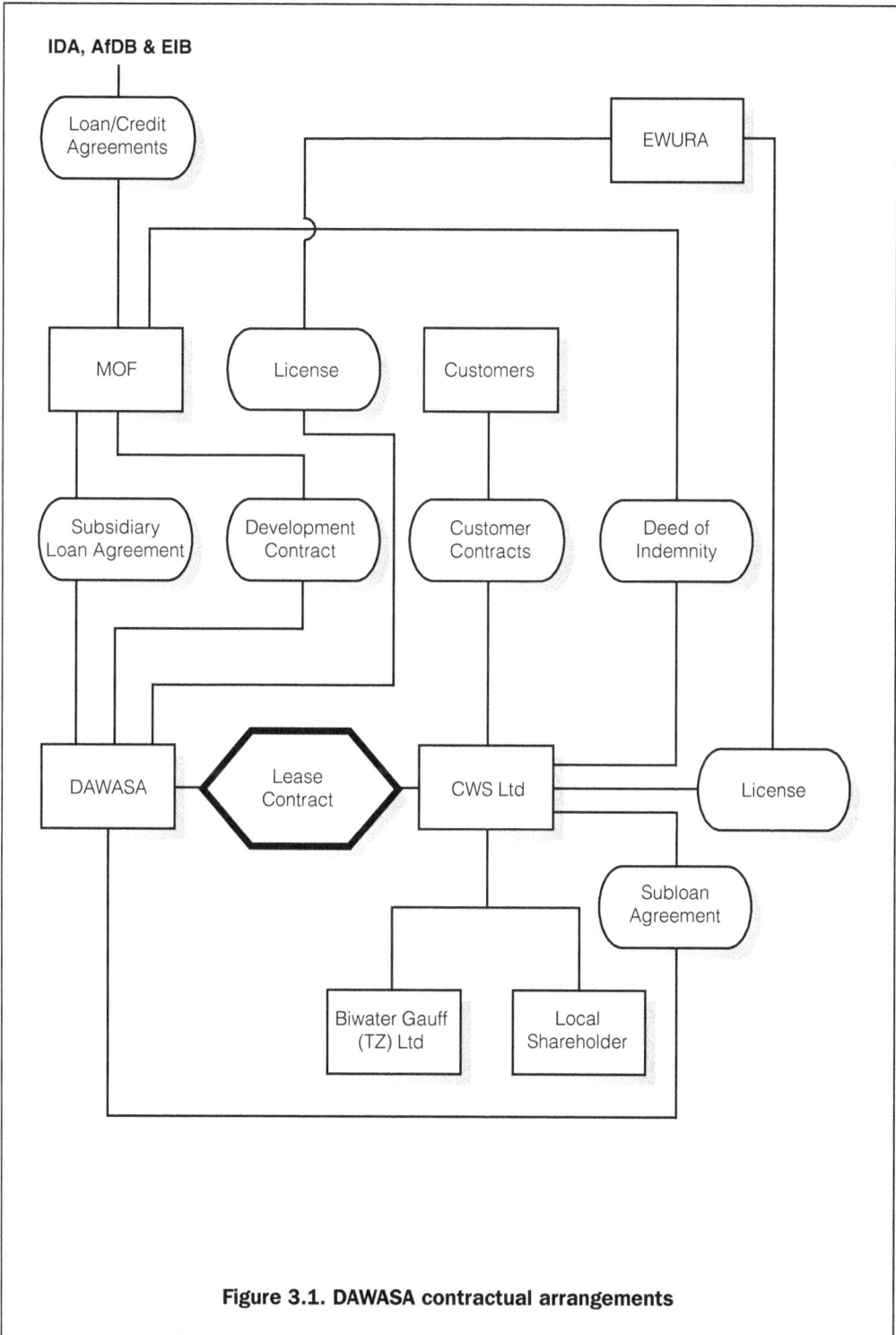

Figure 3.1. DAWASA contractual arrangements

Source: World Bank, 2003b

Tanzania. Some of the primary objectives of establishing TCUs were to ensure party supremacy and mobilize the citizens for community development programmes at the grassroots. TCUs are supposed to be composed of 10 houses; in reality, however, they may reach 40. TCU leaders are like *mtaa* leaders and are elected by the household members in the cell.

The Ward Development Committee (WDC) is responsible for planning and approval of development projects and implementation of council and district directives in the ward. The WDC operates with three to five committees, each one being responsible for specific development issues such as health, education, agriculture or security.

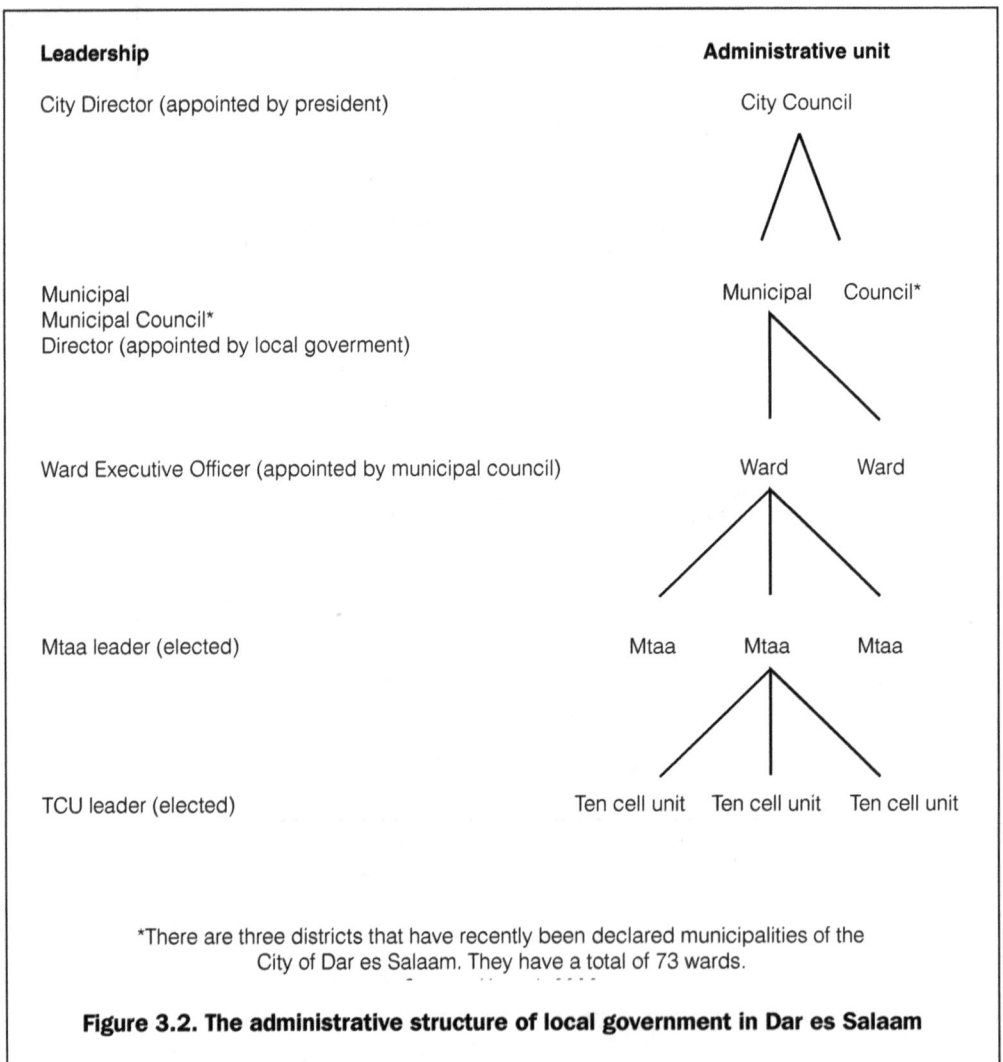

Leadership

City Director (appointed by president)

Municipal
Municipal Council*
Director (appointed by local goverment)

Ward Executive Officer (appointed by municipal council)

Mtaa leader (elected)

TCU leader (elected)

Administrative unit

City Council

Municipal   Council*

Ward   Ward

Mtaa   Mtaa   Mtaa

Ten cell unit   Ten cell unit   Ten cell unit

*There are three districts that have recently been declared municipalities of the City of Dar es Salaam. They have a total of 73 wards.

Figure 3.2. The administrative structure of local government in Dar es Salaam

Source: Kyessi, 2002

```
                    ANNUAL GENERAL MEETING (AGM)


                                                        Board of Trustees
                         Executive Committee


                                                        Consultive Council



  Planning and      Social      Finance and   Technical and   Environment    Poverty
  Co-ordination     Welfare        Admin        Utilities      Committee    Eradication
  Committee        Committee     Committee      Committee                    Committee



  Co-ordinator    Co-ordinator  Co-ordinatior  Co-ordinator  Co-ordinator  Co-ordinator
```

Figure 3.3. Typical organizational structure of a community-based organization

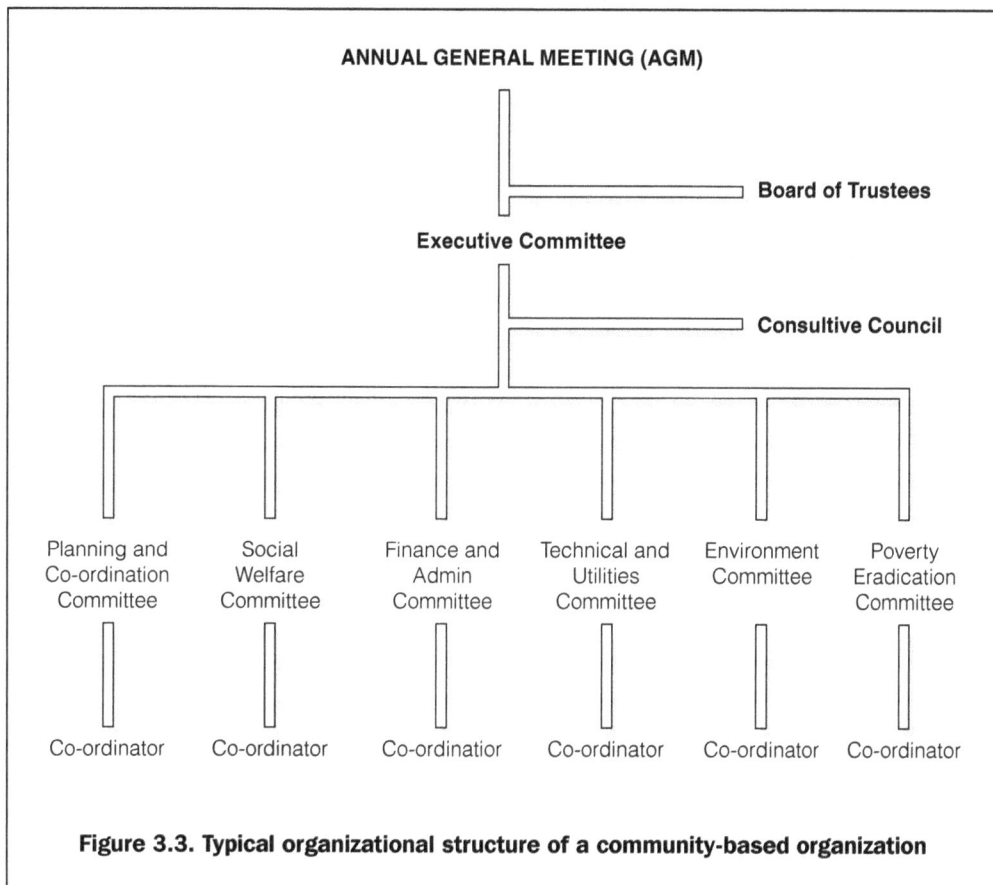

Source: CIP–Dar es Salaam City Council

Informal community structures

There are also informal community structures. These structures are informal in the sense that they are not in the line of local government structures. These are informal community-based organizations for religious, development, and recreational activities, etc. Examples of these groups include the Tabata Development Trust Fund (TDF), Kijitonyama Development Community (KIJIKO), and the Kijichi Development Association (KIBEDEA).

3.3 Legal/regulatory framework

Legal and regulatory framework for urban water supply

Legislation supporting regulations has been enacted at different times to regulate urban water supply programmes. The following legislation was enacted in 1997 to support the decentralization of operations and decision-making:

(a)   Water Use Act (Control and Regulation)
(b)   DAWASA–Miscellaneous Amendment Act Number 18, which amended the National Urban Water Supply Act Number 7 of 1981 to form DAWASA. This was followed by the Water Laws (Miscellaneous Amendments) Act Number 1 of 1999, which made DAWASA comply with the regulatory requirements of EWURA enacted in 2001.
(c)   Waterworks Ordinance, which merged water supply and sewerage under a single authority. The existing legislation however does not address all issues relating to the urban water supply service delivery. The NAWAPO has made a number of provisions for improving water supply. In order to operationalize the policy, a regulatory framework is required to regulate autonomous entities and private sector participation in the delivery of urban water supply services.

Review of existing laws

Thus existing water laws in urban areas are to be broadened, amended and harmonized to accommodate changes that are taking place, including the recent introduction of Energy and Water Utilities Regulatory Authority (EWURA) legislation which has set the broad framework for regulating water and energy services delivery. The laws also need to be reviewed to allow the Ministry of Water and Livestock Development (MoWLD) to continue to regulate the water sector when and where the private sector is not involved as provided for in the policy.

Most of the private boreholes drilled in Dar es Salaam for the purpose of selling water in unserved areas do not have water rights.

At the moment there is inadequate enforcement of the regulations and operational rules governing groundwater use and pollution control. Enforcement of the regulations is needed in order to control over-exploitation and interference in the existing water sources and instead enhance the sustainability of the available groundwater quantity and quality.

The Land Act, 1999 (Act Number 6) allowed houses in informal urban and peri-urban settlements to be accepted as part of the housing stock and integrated into the urban eco system (see Section 5.1).

3.4   Coverage and demand

The water supply service is erratic, with most households getting supply for less than six hours per day. As a result, city-wide water rationing is used to distribute the available supply. Based on the Household Budget Survey of 2000/01, about 85 per cent of the city's households have some kind of access to piped water supply.

However, the World Bank Appraisal (2003b) estimates that 75 per cent of the total population in the service area of about 2.6 million people (2002 population census) get water only a few days per week. More than 45 per cent of households buy water from neighbours, tanker trucks or from vendors. The present production capacity of about 273,000 m³/day from surface water services plus up to 30,000 m³/day from groundwater should be sufficient to supply a city of 3 million, a population Dar es Salaam is likely to reach in 2007. At that time the report estimates that 70 per cent of the serviced area will have a 24-hour service. Apparently, these conditions will be attained after carrying out the planned rehabilitation works, including leakage control measures envisaged under DWSSP.

Service coverage by different sources and suppliers

Service coverage by different providers is reviewed and summarized below based on the data from both recent relevant studies data and this study. Further details are provided in Appendix 3, Table A3.1.

- The population in the Dar es Salaam service area is about 2.6 million: 200,000 in Bagamoyo and Kibaha and 2.4 million in Dar es Salaam.
- The current water production by City Water is 273,450 m³ per day from surface water sources and 30,000 m³ per day from groundwater sources.
- The water leakage in transmission and distribution is estimated at 40 per cent. Thus the water available to consumers is 194,070 m³ per day (assuming negligible water wastage in groundwater supply sources).
- According to City Water records (August, 2004) there are 104,950 connections, of which 95,642 are domestic connections each estimated to serve about 10 people. This makes a total of approximately 1 million people served by direct connections. There are community water supply systems serving approximately 100,000 people and standposts serving about 1 million people (World Bank, 2003b).
- The Bank's appraisal report estimated average household consumption for the city at 6.4 m³/month. Household size is 4.3 people according to 2002 census.
- Based on a population of 2 million people served with house connections and standposts as well as resellers of utility water, a proportion of 85.7 percent of households (HBS, 2002) receive some form of piped supply at estimated daily production of 85,120 m³/day. However, the HBS coverage figure (85.7 per cent) is higher than the 78 per cent coverage estimated by other technical studies in Dar es Salaam.
- The 1 million people directly connected constitute about 42 per cent of the Dar es Salaam population of 2.4 million people. About 100,000 people supplied through communal water supply systems constitute about 4 per cent of the population.

- A study by WSP (WSP, 1999) estimates coverage by tanker trucks at about 2 per cent and by push-cart vendors at 2 per cent.
- The HBS study (2002) estimated water supply coverage through private and public wells at 3.2 per cent and 4.7 per cent respectively, based on a population of 2 million people, whereas the IRC/WSP study coverage was 21.3 per cent (based on borehole production of 32,000 m^3/day) for both private and public wells on the basis of on an estimated population of 3 million for Dar es Salaam.
- Based on the HBS data, the present study estimates the coverage at about 13 per cent through private and communal boreholes based on Dar es Salaam's population of 2.4 million. The increase in borehole water supply coverage, especially in the period after the drought of 1997, is due to increased private investment in borehole water supply in the informal settlements in an effort to fill the supply gap left by the utility.
- The number of people depending on unprotected sources was about 3.5 per cent (HBS, 2002). This coverage has been revised downwards to 2.7 per cent to take into account the increase in borehole water supply coverage in the period after the drought of 1997.
- Based on the above coverage percentages by different service providers, the coverage by utility resellers is estimated at 35 per cent (840,000 people) of the Dar es Salaam population of 2.4 million people.

  Hence, utility water coverage through direct connections is about 42 per cent, communal utility kiosk is 4 per cent, utility water resellers 35 per cent, tanker trucks about 2 per cent, pushcart vendors 2 per cent, private and communal boreholes 13 per cent, as well as about 2 per cent from unprotected sources. Thus the percentage coverage through various vendors is about 56 per cent (see Figure 3.4).

3.5   Existing water sources and supply options

The range of sources or supply options available in Dar es Salaam includes the river, hand-dug wells, rainwater harvesting, private shallow wells with handpumps, communal water boreholes and kiosks, neighbour's piped connections, street water vending, and private water boreholes.

The HBS shows a decline in piped water supply services (in-house, outside house, to neighbour and to the community) and a doubling of households relying on protected and unprotected point sources including private and public wells in the period between 1991–2001 as shown in Table 3.1.

Unprotected sources 2%

Communal kiosks 4%

Pushcart venders 2%

Tanker trucks 2%

Communal and private boreholes 13%

DAWASA 42%

Utility resellers 35%

Figure 3.4. Percentage coverage by various water service providers

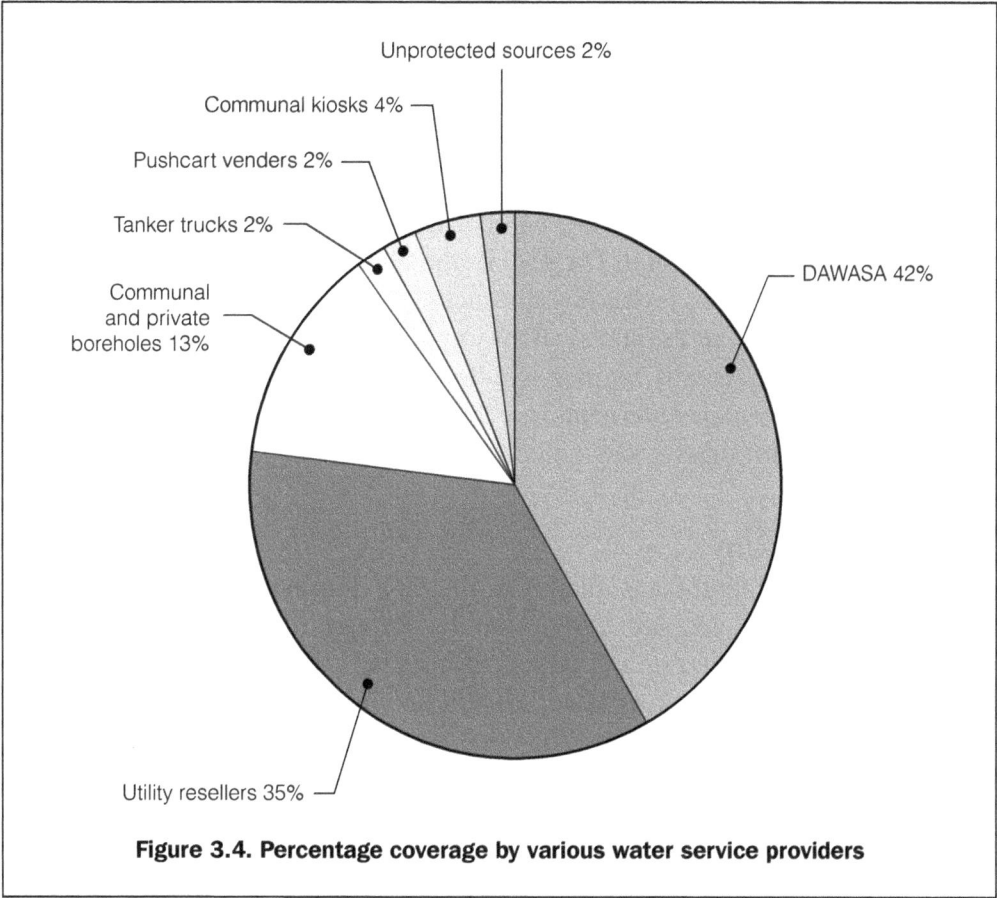

Observations

- The decline in piped water supply services and the rising trend in the use of unprotected point sources is not a favourable water supply situation. These trends imply that unserved low-income people in the informal settlements are the ones most affected by the decline in the delivery of safe and clean water.
- Provision of private wells increased by 700 per cent in the period (1991–2001) as compared to only a 34 per cent increase in public wells, thus indicating a rapid local private sector involvement and injection of local private finance into the water sector in Dar es Salaam. It is also indicative of the as yet untapped local private sector potential for the sector in the informal settlements.

Distance to water source

The 2000–1 HBS also carried out an assessment of distances travelled by households to access water. It covered the entire country including rural areas,

Dar es Salaam, and other urban areas, particularly during the dry season. The results for Dar es Salaam are shown in Table 3.2.

Observations

- The survey shows a decreasing number of households reporting a drinking water source within 1 km in Dar es Salaam during the dry season.
- The survey also shows increasing distances (more than 3 km) to water sources for households in Dar es Salaam. This implies that unserved and inadequately served people, especially women who are charged with fetching water in the low-income informal settlements, are the ones to walk longer distances and to have less time for other social and economic activities.

Groundwater quality

Measurement of groundwater quality in the city indicates that the unconfined aquifer is starting to degrade. More than 40 per cent of groundwater samples analysed for nitrates, chloride and faecal coliform bacteria did not comply with the national standards for drinking water. In addition, groundwater abstraction rates are not adequately regulated. Since demand for groundwater is on the increase in the city, a groundwater management plan is necessary to ensure sustainable use of the resource (Mato, 2003).

Existing and planned borehole sources

The yields and water quality of boreholes drilled in Dar es Salaam in the 1980s and 1990s show that the groundwater potential is greater than earlier estimated by the Dar es Salaam and Coast Regions Water Master Plan in 1979.

Communal and especially private boreholes owned by SWEs (developed following the drought of 1997) are increasingly becoming the major point sources of water supply in the informal settlements.

The specialized non-governmental organizations that are currently helping DAWASA to plan and implement community-managed water supply systems will use boreholes as point sources.

Future source expansion studies

The planned water supply programme includes studies for the selection of future water sources for the DAWASA-designated service area, assessment of the groundwater potential in the area, and the associated comprehensive regional environmental assessment. The studies are scheduled for completion before 2008

Table 3.1. Households' source of drinking water supply in Dar es Salaam		
Source	**1991–2 (%)**	**2000–01 (%)**
Piped water	**93**	**85.7**
Piped water to house	22.1	13.7
Piped outside house (private)	52.6	19.1
Piped to neighbour	NA	46.4
Piped to community	18.4	6.6
Other protected sources	**3.8**	**7.9**
Public wells	3.5	4.7
Private wells	0.4	3.2
Unprotected sources	**1.8**	**3.6**
Public wells	1.7	2.2
Private wells	0.1	1.0
Springs	0	0.2
River, dams, lakes	0	0.1
Other sources	**1.4**	**2.8**

Source: HBS, 2002.

Table 3.2. Distances to drinking water source in Dar es Salaam		
Distribution of distance	**1991–92 Households (%)**	**2000–01 Households (%)**
Less than 1 km	88.5	84
1 – 1.9 km	7.8	6.5
2 – 2.29 km	2.3	1.7
3 – 3.9 km	0.1	3.3
4 – 4.9 km	0.6	2.3
6 km+	0.6	2.2

Source: HBS, 2002.

and the expansion of the sources may commence around 2010 if funds are made available.

Observations

- Following the 1997 drought, communal and especially private boreholes owned by SWEs became the main sources of supply in the informal settlements which are not served or inadequately served by the utility network.
- While plans for the development of future water sources are underway it is important for the utilities (DAWASA, City Water Services and the municipalities) to consider and recognize the private borehole owners who have invested their own funds in the water sector and are now providing point sources near to customers or are delivering piped water services directly to unserved households or delivering indirectly through pushcart vendors. In other words, making the most of the services of private borehole owners (SWEs) gives the utilities a chance to plan and mobilize the resources required to expand existing water sources.
- In the interim, the focus of improvement measures will be on the quality of water from the private boreholes and other related factors, including price of water (discussed later) for the mutual benefit of the communities, utilities and the borehole operators (SWEs). In particular, assessment and regular monitoring of chemical and bacteriological quality of water from boreholes, especially those that are prone to pollution, should be carried out by the municipal health staff.

3.6 Water infrastructure

The Dar es Salaam water supply system supplies the city's urban population. It also supplies people in the rural wards in the northern and western parts of the region, that is in the Kibaha and Bagamoyo administrative districts of the Coast Region that are intersected by the transmission mains from the Ruvu intakes.

The existing waterworks production capacity is 273,000 m^3/day comprised of the Upper Ruvu Plant (82,000 m^3/day), Lower Ruvu Plant (182,000 m^3/day) and Mtoni plant (9,000 m^3/day) – all from surface water – plus up to about 30,000 m^3/day from groundwater (World Bank, 2003b).

The Upper Ruvu plant was rehabilitated in the late 1980s. The Lower Ruvu plant, commissioned in the mid-1970s, requires major rehabilitation. Water losses along the Upper and Lower transmission mains which convey water to the city are high due to weak points in the mains, leading to illegal connections and misuse of water for irrigation purposes.

The primary distribution network is sufficiently developed. However the coverage of the secondary distribution network is limited. Water losses in the water supply system are also high (over 50 per cent unaccounted for water). Although citywide water rationing is practised, many areas are inadequately served or unserved and rely on long and sometimes illegal individual connections. The resulting poor-quality piped system has encouraged very active water vending businesses and the development of boreholes.

Future system expansion studies
Planned medium-term water supply programmes will support studies for expansion of the existing water supply system to meet future water demands in the city, including the informal settlements.

Financing responsibilities
DAWASA is responsible for financing and implementing a five-year capital investment programme under the Dar es Salaam Water Supply and Sanitation Project (DWSSP) which will cost about US$164.6 million. The delegated works will be designed and supervised by a private operator. The operator will also implement a priority works programme to improve water supply system operational efficiency and boost revenue collection. The programme is co-financed by the World Bank, African Development Bank and European Investment Bank.

The programme includes a water supply and sanitation component designed to cater for the needs of low-income people living in unserved or inadequately served peri-urban areas and for communities along the transmission mains that convey water to the city. Four specialized NGOs under the supervision of DAWASA will implement about 40 water supply and 10 sanitation projects using a participatory approach. The water supply projects which will consist of stand-alone borehole water supply systems (borehole and pump, storage tank and supply points or metered bulk supply to communities) which will be managed by through community-based organizations.

Observations
- The completion of project preparation activities for future source and water supply system expansion, along with the timely availability of source and facilities expansion funds (mainly from external sources), will determine when the work can begin. We anticipate that this will happen around 2010.
- In the meantime, measures to improve SWEs' services in the informal settlements will give the government and utilities time to plan and organize resources for system expansion.

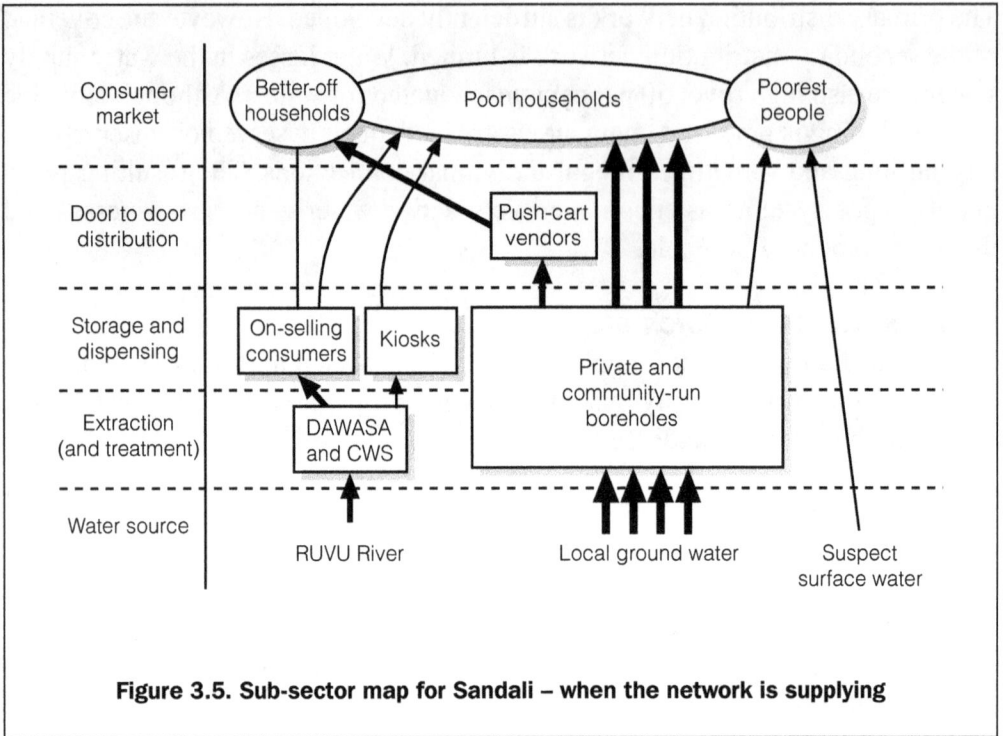

Figure 3.5. Sub-sector map for Sandali – when the network is supplying

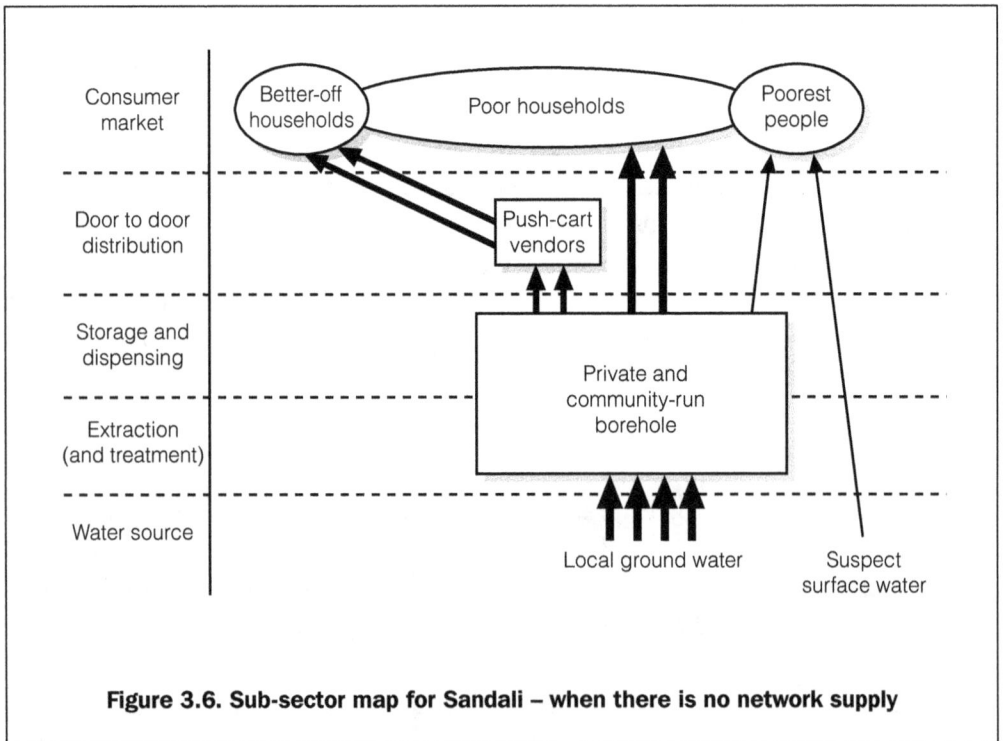

Figure 3.6. Sub-sector map for Sandali – when there is no network supply

3.7 Dar es Salaam city-level water-sector map

Figures 3.2 and 3.3 show sub-sector maps for Sandali in Dar es Salaam, both when the network is providing supplies and when there is no network supply. The figures show water consumers/markets (at the top of the map), functions (water extraction, treatment, transmission, storage and distribution – on the left side), actors (suppliers and distributors – utilities, SWEs, etc. shown in separate boxes) and linkages (shown by arrows). (See also Section 7.3.)

Affordability

The infrastructural and institutional reform measures in Dar es Salaam include the following affordability elements for low-income people:

- Low-income households will be offered low-cost water connections as well as increased access to standposts.
- Low-income households will benefit from a 'lifeline' water tariff that bills consumption of the first 5 m³/month at a lower tariff.
- Communities that cannot initially be served by the distribution network will have access to financing to develop alternative systems (i.e. community-managed water supply systems) and assistance for managing them.

Table 3.3.	Water tariffs in Dar es Salaam	
No.	**Category of consumer**	**TSh/m³**
1	Domestic:	
	First 5m³ consumed each month	337
	Any further amount above 5m³	451
2	Institutional	725
3	Commercial	725
4	Industrial	725
5	Reconnection fee – domestic TSh15,000 plus security, which is equivalent to about three months of water bills.	
	Sewerage charges are linked to water supply charges @ TSh135/m³ (in addition to water charges).	
	VAT is charged as 20 per cent of sewerage charges.	

Source: City Water Services Ltd, 2003.

Price of water
The utility water tariffs are as shown in Table 3.3, (effective 1 August, 2003):

Price of water supplied by vendors
Where vendors with pushcarts or water tankers supply water, consumers pay service charges directly to the supplier. There are a few cases where individuals have developed private water sources like boreholes and shallow wells in areas which are not served by the utility network. Members of this informal private category of suppliers do not have business licences and do not pay for the water abstracted from the ground, nor do they pay the utility anything else. They establish their own water charges individually and sell water to residents, pushcart vendors and water tankers. Similarly the latter two establish their own rates for selling on water. The money collected is used for the operation and maintenance of their water supply systems.

There are several areas where DAWASA has recently dug and equipped deep boreholes that serve communities living near the sources. Such systems are managed by the community through an elected water committee. Groundwater is abstracted free of charge. Water charges are set by the community. Another category of suppliers is that of resellers of utility water. They pay fixed monthly water bills to the utility. The resellers sell water to their neighbours.

Chapter 4

Current Water Policy Issues

4.1 National water policy

The National Water Policy of 1991 emphasized the role of the central government as the sole investor, implementer and manager of projects in urban and rural areas. The government was also responsible for protecting water sources while environmental protection was not accorded its due importance.

The government's overall objective is to improve public health, the environment and to support economic activities in urban areas of Tanzania. The 2002 revised National Water Policy (NAWAPO) is set within the government's overall policy framework of the Poverty Reduction Strategy Paper (PRSP) and Development Vision 2025. It forms an important foundation for meeting the Millennium Development Goals for the water sector, which requires a reduction by half in the number of urban people without access to potable water supply and sanitation services by 2015.

The main objective of NAWAPO is to provide sustainable, reliable and affordable water to all water users in urban and peri-urban areas. The role of the government will shift from providing urban water supply services to facilitating and financing urban water supply services.

The specific objectives of the policy include:

- The creation of an enabling environment and appropriate incentives for the delivery of services, development of an effective decentralized institutional framework that also ensures the autonomy of the water supply and sewerage bodies, and the development of an effective legal and regulatory framework for all sector players, including the private sector.

Observations

- There is, however, no provision for the assessment and recognition of small-scale independent providers in the current water supply programmes in Dar es Salaam as required by the National Water Policy (NAWAPO) (see Section 4.1).
- Based on consultations with City Water Services, private agents will be contracted by the water utility to run 250 water kiosks to be constructed in the unserved low-income areas. This could be the starting point and a good opportunity for interaction between the water utility and the small local private sector (SWEs) in the provision of water supply services in the informal urban settlements.

Policy on sources and infrastructure

As land becomes scarce, urban water sources are becoming vulnerable to the invasion and settlement around them, leading to pollution of the sources. The policy therefore states that:

- Water sources and infrastructure will be identified, protected, demarcated and land title deeds acquired.
- Assessment of land around a source with regard to acquisition of land title will be made prior to applying for a water right.

Observations

- Consultations with the key utility informants revealed that some private boreholes drilled by private drillers in informal settlements were constructed and commissioned without due regard for existing regulations related to the siting and drilling of boreholes, groundwater abstraction, water quality and applications for water rights.
- Consultations with private developers during the study revealed that they were generally unaware of such issues, suggesting that public education on policy issues is necessary.

Policy on financing of urban water supply services

The policy states that urban water supply and sewerage entities are weak in billing, metering, revenue collection, metering water use, and preventing leakages and wasteful use. Among other measures the policy states that private water supply sources in urban areas will not be allowed, except with permission from a legally recognized regulator.

Observation

- The policy statement on private water supply sources in urban areas may constrain small scale private sector participation in the delivery of water supply services, especially to the un-served low-income population in the informal settlements.

Private sector participation

One of the goals of NAWAPO is to have efficient urban water supply and sewerage (UWSS) services through private sector participation.

In order to achieve this goal the policy states that:

- The government will create a conducive environment for the private sector to participate in the delivery of UWSS Services.
- The local private sector will be promoted.
- Existing UWSS infrastructure will be rehabilitated and capacity building undertaken to enable Urban Water Supply and Sewerage Authorities (UWSAs) to operate commercially in order to attract private sector investment.

The policy further states that in order to create a conducive environment for the private sector to participate in the delivery of UWSS services:

(a)   UWSAs will be strengthened to attract private sector participation.
(b)   The capacity of the ministry responsible for water to procure operators, goods and services from private sector will be strengthened.
(c)   Public campaigns to enlighten the public about the objectives of PSP will be conducted.
(d)   Local private sector institutions will be strengthened.
(e)   A regular assessment of private sector performance in the provision of urban water and sewerage services will be instituted.
(f)   Small-scale water supply and sanitation service providers[1] will be assessed and officially recognized.

Observation

- Item (f) allows for the promotion and development of SWEs in the water sector.

Incentives to serve the poor

One of the goals of the water policy is to improve water and sanitation services for low-income groups and community user groups in low-income and peri-urban areas. The policy states that:

- People living in underprivileged urban and peri-urban areas rarely benefit from adequate water supply and sanitation services. They collect water from kiosks or buy it from vendors at a cost higher than that of the house connections.
- Recognizing the existence of low-income groups in the urban and peri-urban areas, UWSS bodies shall be required to provide them with appropriate water supply services.
- Given the importance of water for life and survival, appropriate social equity considerations shall be put in place so that a basic level of water supply service is provided to the poor at affordable cost.
- Entities shall promote workable mechanisms whereby the water supply needs of the urban and peri-urban poor are promoted in all initiatives that encourage public–private partnerships.

Observation

- The last policy statement above concerning public–private partnership offers an opportunity for partnership between the water utilities in Dar es Salaam and the SWEs in the delivery of water supply services, particularly in the informal settlements.

4.2 Utility (DAWASA) policy and strategy for serving the urban poor in Dar es Salaam

The water supply programmes of DAWASA and City Water Services have incorporated the current water policy goals and strategies in the rehabilitation and extension of Dar es Salaam water supply and sanitation infrastructure.

The rehabilitation and extension project is supporting the GoT strategy of focusing first on rehabilitating the existing water supply and sanitation infrastructure and on extending the piped water service to poorly served areas through kiosks to be constructed by the operator (City Water Services) and operated by agents. The water supply component is also supporting a 'Community Water Supply and Sanitation' programme to serve about 40 to 50 low-income communities that may not rapidly benefit from the improved piped water service, either because they are located in remote areas or because the revenue they can generate for the utility is not sufficiently attractive.

The current water supply strategy for low-income households has taken into consideration the affordability of the water supply service as follows:

(a) Low-income households will be offered low-cost water connections as well as increased access to standposts (kiosks) as mentioned earlier.
(b) Low-income households will benefit from a 'lifeline' water tariff that bills consumption of the first 5 m^3/month at a lower tariff.
(c) Communities that cannot initially be served by the distribution network will have access to financing to develop alternative systems (stand-alone borehole water supply systems that are not connected to the existing utility network and metered bulk supply from the utility network), and assistance in managing them using the beneficiary communities themselves.

4.3   Future access to water in informal settlements

The envisaged rehabilitation and extension project for the Dar es Salaam Water Supply and Sanitation Project is estimated to cost about US$164.5 million, of which about US$3 million is earmarked for financing community water supply and sanitation programmes in low-income settlements and an additional amount will finance the installation of 250 kiosks in the unserved low-income areas. It is estimated that these on-going interventions by DAWASA and City Water Services respectively will deliver water to about 350,000 people in the low-income informal settlements by year 2008.[2]

Observations

• Taking into consideration that about 70–75 per cent[3] of Dar es Salaam's 2.4 million people (about 1.68 million people) live in informal settlements, it will take much longer than 2008 to deliver water services to these areas. Thus reliance on the government, external support agencies, and on the international private sector alone will not be sufficient to guarantee a scaling-up of water supply service provision that reaches the poor quickly in the short and medium term.
• There is therefore need to implement the requirements of the water policy by providing an institutional mechanism/framework for attracting, developing and supporting local small-scale water providers that are interested in taking the initiative to invest in small water supply systems for delivering services in the un-served informal settlements. This intervention will help to attract local private sector finance into the water sector to the mutual advantage and benefit of the informal settlement communities, utilities and small-scale local investors.

1. Thus SWEs comprise one category of micro-enterprises under the informal sector. In addition to filling a long-term water supply gap left by the utilities in the low-income settlements, SWEs provide employ-ment. According to the government policy for Small and Medium Enterprises, (SMEs) (Ministry of Industry and Trade, 2003), micro, small and medium-sized enterprises play a crucial role in employment creation and income generation. Out of 700,000 new entrants into the labour force annually, about 660,000 (94 per cent) join the unemployed or underemployed reserve and end up in the SME sector, and especially in the informal sector, generating their own livelihoods. Given that situation and the fact that Tanzania is characterized by low rate of capital formation, SWEs as a sub-component of SMEs need to be supported. Micro-enterprises employ up to four people, mostly family members.

2. Based on discussions held with City Water Services and a review of the World Bank Appraisal report, 250 kiosks are expected to deliver water to about 250,000 people. The 40 DAWASA community water supply projects are expected to deliver water to about 100,000 people (i.e. 2,500 people per project).

3. The National Human Settlements Development Policy (MoLHSD, 2000) estimates that unplanned areas accommodate about 70-75 per cent of the population of Dar es Salaam.

Chapter 5

Informal Urban Settlements

5.1   Informal settlements overview

General overview

The shortage of adequate housing in urban areas, especially in Dar es Salaam, prompted the newly independent government in 1961 to adopt various measures aimed at increasing the supply of adequate housing for city dwellers. The measures ranged from destruction of informal housing to consolidation.

By 1969 the government had realized that the strategy was grossly inappropriate because, among other things, it had resulted in a net reduction in housing stock, while the ability of the government to build new houses to replace and adequately accommodate everyone who was displaced was insufficient. In 1972 the government adopted a new policy towards informal settlement development. The main objective was to recognize the role and existence of informal housing areas and improve them by providing roads, street lighting, piped water, electricity and storm water drainage and by providing community facilities such as schools, health centres and markets. Houses in informal settlements were finally accepted as part of the housing stock and were integrated into the urban ecosystem.

Typology and settlements patterns

About 70 per cent of the population of Dar es Salaam live in unplanned settlements (MoLHSD, 2000). The unplanned settlements in Tanzania do not just house low-income earners; middle-income people also live there due to the lack of plots for development in planned areas. Thus there are unplanned areas with all the usual services such as water, solid waste collection and electricity.

Unplanned/legal

There are quite a few unplanned legal settlements that are officially recognized; the houses are numbered and they pay property tax. Such areas are not prevented from being connected to urban social services such as water and/or electricity provided the primary infrastructure is accessible (see Section 5.1).

Unplanned/illegal

These are typically settlements that are located along river valleys. These settlements are affected by high groundwater table so their sanitation situation is very poor. The conditions become more alarming during the rainy season when floods affect people residing in valleys, to the extent that some even lose their lives.

Planned legal

About 25 per cent of people reside in legal planned urban areas. Such areas include Mikocheni, Msasani, Oysterbay, Kijitonyama and so on. Service delivery in such areas is better than in unplanned settlements though not all of these areas have reliable services. There is no exact data as to what percentage of people receive reliable services, especially in terms of water supply.

The table below shows the typology of settlements.

Table 5.1. Typology of settlements	
Type	**Ward**
Planned / serviced	Central business area and Magomeni, Kijitonyama and Mwenge
Planned / unserviced	Mickocheni, Sinza, Tabata, Mbagala, Kinyerezi, Mbezi-Beach and Temeke Dovya
Unplanned / serviced	Kinondoni-Hananasifu and some parts of Manzese
Unplanned / unserviced	Kimara, Mbezi–Luisi, Tegeta, Boko, Vingunguti and Bunju
Unplanned / legal	Kimara, Mbezi–Luisi, Tegeta, Boko, Vingunguti and Manzese
Unplanned / illegal	Areas located in valleys near the city centre or in other hazardous lands close to infrastructure services and employment, e.g. Msimbazi valley

5.2 Water supply overview

Low-income areas are essentially un-serviced by the utility. Most of the water services available in the low-income areas exist through third-party initiatives. These include vendor-supplied water services on pushcarts, shallow wells belonging to more financially influential residents, and to a limited extent utility water connection in a few residences. These residences do sell water to neighbours and to vendors who subsequently deliver water to areas of shortage.

The poor suffer most because often they have to buy water from vendors who charge higher rates (per bucket of 20 litres) than the official rate charged by the utility. The quality of the water delivered is questionable. Tests carried out recently show that water from these sources is polluted, mainly as a result of faecal contamination.

5.3 Location selection

Selection of informal settlement for the study

Dar es Salaam has three districts/municipalities, namely Kinondoni, Ilala and Temeke. In each municipality there are a number of informal urban settlements.

Within the City of Dar es Salaam there are 54 major informal urban settlements identified by the sustainable Dar es Salaam Project (SDP), (Dar es Salaam City, 1999). The Community Infrastructure Upgrading Study (CIUP, 2002) in Dar es Salaam identified 310 unplanned sub wards in the three municipalities. Out of these wards, a total of 154 were suitable for upgrading. The remaining were not recommended for upgrading because they were on hazardous land, too small, and too poorly built or faced planning restrictions. Taking the above information into consideration, the selection of the informal settlement for the study was made on the basis of discussions held between local study team members and WaterAid and on the basis of consultations made with key informants from utilities and the following criteria from the study's Terms of Reference:

1) Location should be well defined, cohesive and compact to ensure feasible collection of data.
2) Location should be relatively secure in terms of the perceived degree of permanence and/or stability to enable interventions to be introduced.
3) Selection should take into account that Phase 1 research is intended to lay foundation for action research during Phase 2.
4) One location will be selected in the city.

The selection of the low-income settlement also considered the following criteria concerning the settlement's access to water supply.

i) Informal settlements where no piped water connections exist.
ii) Informal settlements with (inconvenient or costly) access to standpipes or other piped supply.
iii) Informal settlements with no effective access to piped water supplies.
iv) Informal settlements with unreliable connections.

In addition, local factors including familiarity of local collaborating research partners with the local water sector issues also influenced the selection of the settlement for the study. In Dar es Salaam, both local and international non-governmental organizations provide water supply services. The international NGOs

Plan International, Care International and WaterAid operate in Ilala, Kinondoni and in Temeke districts/municipalities respectively. Previous and on-going involvement of the local collaborating research partner and coordinator (WaterAid) in water sector activities in the Temeke district influenced the selection of the district/ municipality for this study.

Preliminary discussions were held between the local research team, the operational staff of the water utility (City Water Services), and the key water supply staff of Temeke Municipal Council. Combined with the study team's preliminary field observations and limited discussions held with residents in the identified settlements, as well as the researchers' familiarity with the conditions pertaining to such low-income settlements, the study team felt that the typology of settlement and water supply service conditions prevailing in Sandali and Yombo Vituka wards were more consistent with the demands of the study. However, priority was given to Sandali Ward because it has a sub-ward which receives very intermittent utility supply and in general the entire ward is served by many alternative water vending sources/supply options. Relevant comparative data for both Sandali and Yombo Vituka are provided in Table 5.2 below as obtained from the ward offices.

The selected study area (Sandali Ward) was not a random sample of low-income informal settlements in Dar es Salaam. Since the study also focused on access to water in the informal settlements through support to SWEs, it was judged necessary to identify and select settlements that substantially responded to the demands (low-income informal settlement with little or no utility supply) of the study.

Overview of the study area

The study was carried out in the five sub-wards of Sandali Ward (previously known as Temeke Mikoroshini), in the Temeke Municipality in the southern part of Dar es Salaam. The whole study area is an informal settlement occupied by low-income residents. The sub-wards are Mamboleo A, Mamboleo B, Sandal, Mwembeladu and Mpogo. They have a total population of 38,631 based on the 2002 Census. The study area is located close to Mandela Road to the north, Nyerere Road to the west, and Maguruwe Road to the east.

Socio-economic characteristics

The main sources of income for most households in the study area are petty trade and paid employment in either central and local government offices or public and private institutions and industries. Petty trade is mainly in foodstuffs which are sold in small market stalls in the area. Domestic consumables such as maize flour, rice, sugar, kerosene, matchboxes, cigarettes, soap, cooking oil, etc. are sold in numerous small shops. A few people, especially men, sell second-hand

Table 5.2. **Selected socio-economic characteristics of Sandali and Yombo Vituka wards**

Informal settlement	Income status	Ward	Mtaa	Population	Water service access	Water vending rating
Sandali ward (Temeke Mikoroshin)	Low	Sandali	Sandali	11,443	Very limited public network	Very high and characterized by the presence of water providing individuals and small informal water providing enterprises, namely water collectors, private borehole owners, boreholes managed by community, street water vendors, private kiosk owners and household resellers of utility water
			Mwembeladu	5,217		
			Mamboleo A	13,198	Very inadequate and intermittent supply	
			Mamboleo B	5,200		
			Mpogo	3,573		
			Total	**38,6311**[†]		
Yombo Vituka	Low	Yombo Vituka	B. Mwinyi	10,110	No public network	Very high and characterized by presence of water collectors, private boreholes owners, boreholes managed by community and street water vendors
			Kilakala	14,464	Supply comes from shallow boreholes/ wells owned by individuals or managed by communities	
			Vituka	11,499		
			Sigara	8,280		
			Machimbo	15,428		
			Total	**59,7812**[††]		

Sandali area, within Temeke District, was previously known as 'Temeke Mikoroshini'.
[†] Year 2002 census gives ward population figure of 39,136 for Sandali
[††] Year 2002 census population figure is 59,975
Note: The population of Temeke District (urban and rural) is 771,500 (2002 Census).

Source: Sandali Ward Office; 2003.

clothes, make and repair shoes and clothes, repair cars, sell water, operate small welding works, or make furniture to sell locally. Some of the women are involved in sewing, embroidery, mat-making, tailoring, preparing and selling food by the roadside and brewing local beer.

Most food is bought from market stalls as there is no significant agricultural activity in the area. The congestion and haphazard building of houses in the settlement does not leave enough space to grow vegetables for household use. The major staples are maize meal (known as ugali in Swahili) and rice supplemented with cassava, potatoes, and bananas and plantains.

The people in the study area are affected by a number of diseases including malaria, diarrhoea, dysentery, cholera, HIV/AIDS, tuberculosis, and malnutrition, among others.

The settlement pattern of the study area and services

- Settlements are characterized by a lack of order in the layout of buildings, the lack of drainage system, congestion, the lack of recreational grounds, etc. The area is generally accessible by road.
- The houses are made of cement brick walls or poles/mud/mud plaster walls with corrugated iron sheet roofs and cement or earth floors.
- There is one primary school, and there are small dispensaries, small police posts and places of worship.
- Only small parts of the Mwembeladu and Sandali sub-wards are served with a public utility water supply and that is rationed and intermittent. Pit latrines are widely used. Solid waste collection is carried out by private companies but their service at the time of the study was irregular. Electricity and telephone services are also available.
- For the majority of people in the study area the main energy source for cooking is charcoal which is produced in the hinterland of Dar es Salaam. Charcoal is preferred to firewood because it is easier to handle.
- The area is earmarked for infrastructure upgrading (roads, drainage, water supply, sanitation, etc.) under a World Bank-funded Community Infrastructure Upgrading Programme (CIUP).

Water supply service in the study areas

The only surface water source in the area is the Yombo River which is heavily polluted by industrial wastewater discharges from industries located on the Nyerere Road to the north of the settlement. Only small areas of the Mwembeladu and

Sandali sub-wards have piped utility water. The supply is unreliable and only available during the night twice a week. This situation has created an environment conducive to street water vending and the reselling of utility water by neighbours with piped connections. The other sub-wards have no piped water. Most of the residents in all the wards rely mainly on private boreholes (see the Inventory of Boreholes in Mamboleo A, Mamboleo B and Mpogo sub-wards in Appendix 5), community-managed boreholes constructed by either DAWASA or Temeke municipality, as well as on municipal wells with handpumps whose supply is seasonal and quality is questionable because of the high pollution potential from the wide use of pit latrines in the area. Some hand-dug wells are located in the riverbed of the polluted Yombo River.

In the entire ward there are many pushcart water vendors who go around selling water in 20-litre jerrycans. Rainwater harvesting is practised but because of inadequate storage facilities not much water is stored.

Utility customers in the study area
During the study, efforts were made to (a) identify the registered utility customers in Sandali ward in the customer billing records kept at the City Water Services – Temeke Office and (b) locate the customers on the utility maps and in the field. This exercise did not yield the desired customer information data because the customers on the billing records could not be identified/traced to a specific supply area/sub-ward in the study settlement. The name of the ward itself (Sandali) and those of its sub-wards (Sandali, Mwembeladu, Mamboleo A, Mamboleo B and Mpogo) did not exist in the billing records examined.

The name Temeke Mikoroshini – which is the former name for the Sandali area – is still used in the billing records. According to the records, Temeke Mikoroshini is also referred to interchangeably as Temeke kwa Maganga or Tandika Mikoroshini.

A sample monthly payment trend of water supply customers for the months of March and April 2004 in the settlement was extracted from the City Water Account Code Numbers 231 and 232. Only eight customers from the study area settled their bills with City Water Services in April 2004. There were 12 payments for March 2004. This information, however, does not give a good indication of the number of water supply customers in the area.

Discussions held with City Water Services staff confirmed that the water supply service in the area had been unreliable for a long time and that the customer information database was also out of date.

Observation

For the utility to know its customers in the study area and to improve both water supply services (under the CIUP and future extensions) and billing and revenue collection, a house-to-house survey would be required to identify and confirm the total number and particulars of the customers in the billing records and to locate them on utility maps and in the field.

Chapter 6

Water Services and Poverty

6.1 Methodology

A review of secondary information, including individual household interviews and focus group discussions, was held with 20 households and five focus groups in order to get information on water services and poverty in the study area.

6.2 Household employment, income and water expenditure

Many of the households interviewed were male-headed and consisted of five to seven people. Consumers' income is one of the main factors influencing people's ability to pay for water supply services. The study attempted to establish the main sources of household monthly income and the extent to which water expenditure contributes to monthly household expenditure.

The interviews revealed that very few people are employed in government or private offices. Most of those who are employed are men who work as security guards, labourers in godowns (warehouses), and masons and carpenters working for private construction companies, mainly outside the study settlement.

The women work in their homes and also engage in small petty trading outside. Such activities include selling fruit, vegetables, buns, etc. and tailoring clothes for individual customers. According to the women's group discussions these commodities and services do not sell particularly well because people cannot afford them. The average monthly income of many of the households interviewed was TSh40,000.

Household expenditure on water ranged between TSh150 and TSh200 per day or an average of TSh5,250 per month. Thus about 13 per cent of household income is spent on water. This means households are paying high prices to SWEs for the minimum requirements to ensure their family's survival.

Separate focus group discussions consisting of representatives of women, men, and primary school children were held. The focus groups included owners of informal and formal micro-enterprises, the lowest income group as perceived by the people in the informal settlement. See Appendix 1 for more details of the focus group discussions, which revealed that:

- Life in the informal settlement is difficult.
- Informal petty businesses did not bring in returns because of the low purchasing power of most of the people in the settlement. There were too few customers with good purchasing power and household income was too low to allow higher investment in any petty trade.
- Women selling fruit and vegetables were often forced out of business because these food items rot if not sold quickly.

Observations

The high percentage of household income spent on water is at the expense of the household food budget (see Section 6.2 below). Any intervention which reduces the cost of water to poor households will have an impact on improving household nutrition and hence health. Such interventions might include:

- More accessible utility piped water for poor households through kiosks.
- Installation of more kiosks, thus reducing travelling distance and queuing time for vendors, which will reduce water prices to consumers.

Income groups and poverty

Focus group discussions showed that poverty in the settlement meant that residents suffered high levels of crime. A large number of young people – mostly unemployed men over 18 – were involved in illegal activities, such as theft and robbery, even during the day. During the study period the study team saw armed plainclothes policemen hunting for this group of criminals.

According to the focus group perceptions there were three household income groups in the settlement, as shown in Table 6.1 below.

- People in the high-income group own good houses with security fences and personal cars, can send their children to school, and are guaranteed three good meals a day.
- People in the middle-income group own a house, are guaranteed meals, can rent out part of their house, and can send their children to school.
- People in the low-income group are not sure of earning a daily income, eat a single meal a day, cannot afford to send their children to school, and rent in very poor and insecure shelter with mud or unplastered walls and they do not have corrugated iron sheets for their roof.

Table 6.1. Distribution of income groups as perceived by focus groups

Income groups as defined by focus groups	Male focus group	Female focus group	Primary schoolchildren focus group	Total	Average
Low income (%)	85	45	90	220	73.3
Medium income (%)	10	30	8	48	16.0
High income (%)	5	25	2	32	10.7

- The focus group meetings classified the households on the basis of number of meals per day. The people representing the poorest community members (as defined by the community) said that the number of households based on the number of meals per day were as follows three meals (5 per cent); two meals (30 per cent); one meal (40 per cent) and zero meals (25 per cent). According to the groups a 'zero meal' often means a small piece of roasted cassava spiced with salt and pepper eaten with water.

Perceived problems in the settlement
The focus group discussions also revealed the following problems in the settlement:

- low status of basic education
- most people have low incomes
- low knowledge about planning ahead
- primary school is unaffordable
- water is unavailable
- frequent power supply interruptions
- low level of employment
- public hospital is far away
- one primary school only (recently constructed)
- school is not supplied with water, creating an unhealthy situation for the schoolchildren, who use pit latrines
- theft and robbery is increasing, causing increasing insecurity, especially for the women in the area, both day and night

Prioritized perceived problems
The perceived problems as prioritized by the focus groups are:

1) Non-availability of water in households and schools
2) Public hospital is far away

3)   Roads in the settlement are not maintained
4)   Lack of environmental sanitation (wastewater disposal)
5)   High unemployment for young people

6.3   Patterns of water usage

Different sources of water

The different sources of water used by homeowners and tenants include private connections, water from neighbours' private connection, community-managed borehole water supply system, private borehole water supply system, community-managed kiosk, street water vendors, surface sources (river), shallow wells, and rainwater catchments.

The majority of households do not have piped water connections nor do they have a standpipe in the yard or a utility kiosk in the vicinity of the household.

Those houses that do not have piped water connected to their homes obtain it from a neighbour who is connected to the water supply network or they depend on one or more of the above-mentioned sources. Surface sources are not used much because they are polluted.

Observation
The priority accorded to neighbour's piped water is an indication of the households' preference for utility water services.

Cost of water provided by SWEs

All households which draw water from any source except from the polluted nearby river, open wells located in the river bed, or rainwater catchment pay for their water.

Payment for water is made to different organizations and individuals depending on the source of the water. Almost all households pay for water. Owners and tenant's households with a private piped water connection usually pay monthly bills to the City Water Services. There are very few such households and they are located in Mwembeladu and Sandali sub-wards. Water bills are sent by the utility every month. The monthly assessed bill is about TSh12,000. Households that do not have a water connection but buy water from a neighbour with a private water connection pay the neighbour TSh20 per 20-litre jerrycan on the spot after collecting the water.

The majority of the other households in Mwembeladu and Sandali and in the other three sub-wards usually buy water from street vendors, or directly from private or community-managed boreholes.

Private tanker trucks (water bowsers) rarely supply water to the informal settlement. They more often collect water from the private boreholes to supply un-served wealthier areas like Tabata and Msasani, which are located far away from the informal settlement. The purchase price at the source ranges from TSh5,000 to TSh6,000 for 7,000 to 10,000 litres, and the sale price ranges from TSh45,000 to TSh50,000 – about eight times the purchase price.

The price per 20-litre jerrycan charged by the street water vendors ranges between TSh70 and TSh100. The purchase price at the source ranges between TSh20 and 30. (The higher price is charged by borehole owners during periods of public power supply interruptions, in which case the borehole operator uses a private standby power generator to ensure continuity of water supply to customers.)

Water availability

Utility piped supply serves only a very small area of the Mwembeladu and Sandali sub-wards where the supply is intermittent. The supply situation improves during the rainy season (March–May) and becomes worse during utility pipe bursts, power supply interruptions at the utility sources, and during the dry season (October–January) when utility river water source levels fall below the minimum.

Some of the groundwater sources in the settlement are saline. The women interviewed prefer to travel longer distances and spending more time to collect drinking water that is not salty. The two main water collection periods for women are between 5 and 8am and 4 and 7pm. Most households interviewed had a return journey (walk to source, queue at source, return from source) time of 15 minutes to two hours.

The reliability and sustainability of the supply from the privately owned borehole is generally high according to the experience and perception of the respondents. For example, they said that the supply from the Development Youth Centre borehole in Sandali sub-ward, which is owned and managed by a Roman Catholic Mission, has water of good quality, supplied to consumers through two metered kiosks whose surroundings are well drained and kept clean all the time. The price is fixed at TSh20 per 20-litre jerrycan and does not fluctuate with changing circumstances or seasons. The study team confirmed this information at the centre. The borehole, which was drilled by DDCA, has good water quality (approved by the Ministry of Water Central Laboratory), high-rise water storage tanks with enough capacity to balance water supply requirements in the surrounding area, and a standby electricity generator to ensure a continuous power supply.

Water demand and price

The amount of water ultimately demanded by household consumers depends on the above factors, which are underpinned by price. The respondents were also willing to pay more to street water vendors for water collected from these far-away piped sources. The price charged for a 20-litre jerrycan of water at a borehole source was TSh20 even if the water from the source is salty.

However during power supply interruptions – which are common in the area due to general low power supply voltage – the private borehole owners with standby generators charge TSh30 for a 20-litre jerrycan of water.

How water is used in the settlement

Water use in the settlement is divided into domestic water use (water for drinking, cooking, bathing and cleaning cooking utensils, cleaning house and washing clothes) and for informal and formal micro-enterprises (food vendors, known as *'mama lishe'*, local brewers, guest houses and restaurants).

The households in the study settlement have a variety of water sources available to them, each with different characteristics. Different sources are selected for different water uses. The household water demand is therefore an aggregation of individual requirements for different water uses.

6.4   Coping strategies

Water for drinking and cooking and water for bathing and cleaning clothes and the house is generally collected from different sources. Water for drinking and cooking is usually collected from water sources with water that tastes good, namely utility pipe sources or privately owned boreholes, community-managed boreholes or community-managed utility kiosks. Water for the other uses is often collected from boreholes or shallow well sources with salty water. Most of the residents interviewed complained that water for washing clothes that is collected from salty sources consumes excessive amounts of soap, forcing them to use more expensive powdered soap (detergent) instead.

Many of the households interviewed consume about five or six 20-litre jerrycans of water (100 to 120 litres) per day. The average household size is six people.

According to the 2002 Census the average household size in Dar es Salaam is 4.2 and in Sandali ward 4.0. This family size is slightly smaller than the household size for those interviewed.

Washing clothes and cleaning household utensils consumes about five jerrycans of water per day, so households opt to wash their clothes once a week as a way of reducing water consumption and cost.

Households consume the least amount of water (three jerrycans per day) for drinking and cooking purposes. For health reasons, many of the women interviewed prefer good quality water for drinking and cooking purposes and they are even willing to pay more for it.

- Women, especially the more financially vulnerable ones, fetch water from the sources themselves in order to save money.
- Some households have purchased water supply pushcarts for household use in order to save the money they would otherwise pay to vendors.

According to the households interviewed, if the existing supply is increased and affordable they will: use more water for drinking, cooking and washing; take a bath, clean their clothes and clean their houses more frequently; and start small vegetable and flower gardens around their houses (where space is available).

Observations

Overall, water quality, especially that of utility water, is very much valued by households. This is why women and children are willing to travel longer distances and spend more time to fetch utility piped water and also pay more money for the same amount when delivered to the household by vendors (see Section 6.3).

6.5 Water and health implications

- Households' perceptions of the quality of the water source greatly influence their choice of source. Water collected by households from either surface sources or even protected shallow wells is not generally used for drinking. This is a reflection of the awareness of the people, especially women, concerning the poor quality of water obtained from these sources.
- Water that tastes good (i.e. is not salty), is clear, and does not leave soil particles at the bottom of a glass container when stored for a day or two is generally perceived by the respondents interviewed to be water of good quality.
- The bacteriological quality and other chemical characteristics of the water are not issues of major concern to many of the households interviewed, although they were bitterly concerned about the quality of water supplied from private boreholes located in the vicinity of pit latrines (which is the major means of sanitation in the settlement). The links between water, sanitation and hygiene are not fully understood by the residents, although they associate poor water quality with contamination from nearby latrines. An element of community hygiene education/awareness is required to safeguard the well being of the residents.
- Information on the quality of the water collected from the existing sources is rarely collected and assessed except during cholera epidemics, which are

common in the settlement. During cholera epidemics Temeke Municipal health workers usually take water samples from various sources to determine the quality of water being supplied. A private borehole owner was reportedly stopped by municipal health authorities from supplying water until he added chlorine to the supply in order to disinfect it and make it safe for household consumption.

• There is no institutional mechanism for carrying out routine assessment and monitoring of water quality at the supply sources, during transportation, or when stored at home in household containers.

• Water quality data and approvals for quality compliance of boreholes and related borehole information (borehole logging) for those boreholes drilled by the Drilling and Dam Construction Agency (DDCA) of the Ministry of Water & Livestock Development was given to the study team by some of the borehole owners. For boreholes drilled by private drillers such data were available but lacked detail.

Conclusions on perceived water quality

Water quality monitoring and control is only one factor in the reduction of water-related diseases, but it is an important factor. The execution of water quality surveys in the settlement could help identify those sources that are prone to contamination and require high priority attention.

The quality of water is determined by physical, microbiological, and chemical factors. Physical factors include taste, smell, colour and turbidity.

The physical aspect and whether the water tastes good or salty is what the residents in the settlement often perceive to be the most important, because it is what they use to compare one sort of water with another.

The consumers' perceptions about water quality are also linked to the cleanliness of the vendors and of the water transporting jerrycans.

Microbiological contamination of water – which is due to organisms such as bacteria that are invisible to the naked eye – is not examined on routine basis. These disease-causing organisms could originate from the extensive use of pit latrines in the settlement, as they can infiltrate into the groundwater.

It is recommended that an intervention be carried out that would involve a combination of observation, local knowledge and regular water tests to give information on the quantity and quality of the water in the field. The Temeke Municipality should have qualified staff and enough equipment and facilities to carry out the work. In the interim, water for drinking purposes collected from any source should invariably be boiled.

It should also be appreciated that under the conditions prevailing in the unserved informal settlements water that is safe at the point of delivery can nevertheless present a significant health risk due to contamination during collection, transportation, storage and drawing. Steps that can be taken to minimize such risk include improved collection and storage practices, appropriate collection and storage containers, treatment with a residual disinfectant, or treatment at the households (boiling of the water is the cheapest option at the household). A sanitary survey is recommended to assess the conditions and practices that may constitute a public health risk in the study settlement and to suggest ways to reduce these risks.

Chapter 7

Small Water Enterprises

7.1   Methodology

The study team carried out intensive in-depth interviews with twelve SWEs operating in different parts of the City – six in Sandali Ward, one in Yombo Vituka, two in Mtoni Ward and one each in Azimio, Kurasini and Buguruni. They are all serving market segments (see methodology in Appendix 1). The team also carried out five focus group meetings – three in Sandali Ward and one meeting each in Yombo Vituka and Mtoni Wards – with several SWEs to explore important issues and also to check that initial interviews with individual SWEs were representative. The weaknesses as reported by the SWEs are presented, analysed and grouped under specific problem categories in Section 7.4.

7.2   SWEs overview

The water supply sector in Sandali ward is comprised of small informal water enterprises including street water vendors, private borehole owners, communal water supply boreholes and kiosks, and household resellers of water from the utility network.

Some private borehole owners in Sandali supply piped water through kiosks located at some distance from the borehole point source.

In other areas outside Sandali ward, there are examples of private borehole owners supplying water through a distribution network connected to households and kiosks as well as private borehole owners who are also wholesale transporters.

7.3   Supply chains in the settlement

A 'supply chain' is the term used in this report for the process that relates all activities involved in the flow of water from the source through to the end-user, as well as the associated information flows.

In the study settlement, water and associated services are supplied to customers through different supply chains, from service providers with different water supply sources and options through direct collection and transport by the consumers themselves, through private piped systems or street water vendors who transport the water in jerrycans loaded on pushcarts. Payment flows in the opposite direction.

The basic components of the supply chain are given below:

Water suppliers
Water suppliers include: utilities (DAWASA, City Water Services, municipalities), private borehole owners, community-managed boreholes, and kiosks and resellers of utility water.

Water distributors
Water distributors include:

- Street water vendors, who usually transport six 20-litre jerrycans using pushcarts. They are both retailers and wholesalers of water. Payment is usually made on the spot whenever water is delivered to a customer, or on a monthly basis for a few special customers.
- Water tankers (of 7,000–10,000 litres capacity) transport water which is usually sold wholesale to wealthier households located away from informal settlements. Water is also delivered wholesale to construction sites. Payment is made on delivery or on a monthly basis.

Customers
SWEs' customers in the informal settlements include households and small businesses that use water (local brewers, local food vendors, restaurants, guest houses). Wealthier families living in high-income areas (located far away from the study settlement) without adequate supply purchase water from tankers.

The supply chains in the settlement and the indicative cost per cubic metre of water delivered to the consumer in each supply chain are summarized in Table 7.1.

Observations

- All supply chains in Table 7.1 are important for different consumer segments: those both inside and outside the study settlement, at different distances from sources, and for different supply situations and seasons.
- All the supply chains in the table are used in the settlements studied except for Numbers 7 and 8, where tankers supply water to middle- and high-income people in planned settlements located far away from the informal settlements.
- When a vendor or tanker is used in a supply chain the cost to the consumer increases due to transportation costs. Consumers can reduce costs by excluding

pushcart vendors from the supply chain when and where they find it appropriate to collect water directly from the source if the source is near (Supply chain Numbers 4, 3 and 6). However, if the preferred source (utility piped – especially for drinking water use) is far from the household or if a distant piped source is to be used during the dry season or during periods of water shortages caused by mechanical /electrical failure in the utility system, then vendors becomes necessary.

- It is difficult for the high- and middle-income people to do without the tankers that provide bulk supplies from distant sources to their households. Transportation costs could be reduced by providing more utility kiosks for tankers closer to the beneficiary households. The existing three utility kiosks are inadequate in terms of both service provision and location.

- The minimum cost to the consumer is TSh685/m³ through supply chain Number 1 (Surface source → City Water → communal kiosk → consumer. However the study findings revealed that community-managed kiosks suffer from financial and management problems. Community kiosks managed by private local operators or agents are a more feasible management option to ensure sustainable management of the infrastructure and services.

Table 7.1. Types of supply chain in the study area			
Supply c hain	**Description of supply chain**	**Indicative cost† to consumer per m³ of water (TSh)**	**Remarks**
1) Surface water → City Water → communal kiosk → consumer	A suitable supply chain for the study settlement.	685	Lowest cost water supply chain: based on flat rate tariff of TSh12,000/ month in the study area.
2) Surface water → City Water → communal kiosk → pushcart vendor → consumer	Long supply chain, and water quality is good.	3,205	High-cost water chain; cost could be reduced by increasing number of kiosks and therefore reducing travel distance and cost.
3) Surface water → City Water → utility water reseller → consumer	Supply chain is used in both medium and low-income areas where the number of connected households is low.	1,455	
† Capital investment cost included.			

(Table 7.1. continued on next page)

		Indicative cost[†]	
Supply chain	**Description of supply chain**	**to consumer per m³ of water (TSh)**	**Remarks**
4) Surface water → City Water → utility water reseller → pushcart vendor → consumer	Long supply chain used in study settlement, but important in terms of good quality water.	5,185	Highest cost water supply chain; cost could be reduced by installation of utility kiosks in the study area.
5) Aquifer → private borehole → tanker truck → consumer	Suitable in high and medium-income households where access by road is good.	4,705	High-cost supply chain.
6) Surface water → City Water → city water kiosk → tanker truck → consumer	Common in planned areas (high and medium-income households) where water is transported by road. Also suitable during water shortages.	4,841	High-cost supply chain; cost could be reduced by increasing number of utility kiosks in the neighbourhood of service area to minimize travel distance and cost to consumers.
7) Aquifer → communal boreholes → consumer	Important supply chain in terms of affordability. Suffers financial and management problems, hence poor sustainability.	997	Second-lowest-cost water supply chain.
8) Aquifer → private boreholes → consumer	Important in volume terms: used and accepted in the study settlement; is reliable, affordable and sustainable.	1,194	Third-lowest-cost water supply chain.
9) Aquifer → private borehole → pushcart vendor → consumer	Important in study area in terms of volume and reliability of supply at source.	4,924	High-cost water supply chain; cost could be reduced by extending pipe network with kiosks in the neighbourhood.

Table 7.1.   Types of supply chain in the study area (continued)

[†]   Capital investment cost included.

7.4 Livelihoods of SWE operators

The SWEs interviewed provided information about their businesses and livelihoods. Greater coverage is given to street water vendors in this chapter. The other groups of SWEs are discussed in greater detail in subsequent chapters.

Employment

Street water vending is creating employment mainly for young unemployed men between 18 and 30 years old. Most of the vendors interviewed had been in the business since the early or mid-1990s. One of them has been a water vendor since 1987.

Street water vending is also providing employment for two men who are over 50 and one lady in Mtoni Ward. One of the old men interviewed had been in the business for four years. Previously he was employed in a local industry as a craftsman. According to focus group discussions held in the SWE study areas:

- Young vendors sell more water since they are younger, stronger and can push the carts faster over longer distances than the old men.
- The lady operating in the vending business owns a pushcart that carries six 20-litre jerrycans.
- A few young women (18 years old and above) are employed to work at community-managed boreholes as attendants to operate the systems and collect revenue.
- Selling water at private boreholes and kiosks is mostly done by the family or household members of the owner, especially the housewife and children, but also by paid attendants.

Sources of supply

- The vendors interviewed supply utility water or water from boreholes to meet the type of water preferred by individual customers. They travel and collect utility water from distant supply points. At the supply points, water vendors and other customers (mostly women) are required to join one of two separate queues. Purchase price at the source for all customers is TSh20 per 20-litre jerrycan. Pushcart vendors are often offered a price of TSh100 for six jerrycans, however –a bonus of one free jerrycan. Vendors move from one source to another depending on the type of water demanded by their customers and the price and other incentives offered at a particular source.
- Water collected from boreholes is sold at TSh50–100 per 20-litre jerrycan, while the same amount of water from a utility pipe is sold at TSh100–150. In most cases customer pay on delivery. Billed regular monthly customers are often

offered a lower price of TSh50 per 20-litre jerrycan, depending on the source of water used and the distance to the source.

Technology

- Vendors prefer pushcarts which can carry six 20-litre jerrycans. Bigger pushcarts which accommodate eight jerrycans or more are heavier and difficult for one person to push over a long distance. The pushcarts are manufactured locally in the study area.

Competition among SWEs

Street water vendors face competition from other suppliers:

- Owners of private boreholes, shallow wells and resellers of utility water deliberately reduce prices at the sources in order to attract more household customers, especially women, to collect water directly from the sources.
- Young vendors who are not married – and especially those who are still living in their parents homes – often lower prices, something which the older men in the business would not do due to greater financial obligations to their families.
- According to the street water vendors interviewed, their number of customers has been decreasing due to the greater number of communal and private boreholes which sell water at TSh10-20 per 20-litre jerrycan at the source.
- Previously, vendors rented pushcarts at TSh500 per day. The practice of renting pushcarts has recently decreased because the street water vendors earn less profit while renting pushcarts and so prefer to buy their own instead from local manufacturers.
- There is also no sharing of facilities among the vendors. In conclusion the vendors noted 'Street water vending business is generally satisfactory in terms of giving us livelihood'.

Characteristics of SWEs

The characteristics of the different SWEs studied are described in Table 7.2 with respect to type and quality of service offered, supply area, competition forces in the market and price.

Constraints facing SWEs

The constraints facing SWEs were obtained from different groups of SWEs (private and communal boreholes and street water vendors) and are summarized in Table 7.3.

Perspective of SWEs of their own situation

The constraints facing SWEs are grouped as shown in Table 7.4.

Table 7.2. Characteristics of SWEs					
Potable water operators	Type of service and area of operation in informal settlement	Relative quality of service	Competition for market	Price	
				TSh/20-litre jerrycan	TSh/m³
Connected resellers					
Water is sold directly from private connection linked to DAWASA mains.	Water is good quality in varying quantities. Water is collected into and sold from ground storage tanks. Areas with few household connections receive intermittent utility supply. Payment is made on the spot.	Good quality potable water; supply depends on utility supply cycle / rationing pattern. Quality of water depends on regular cleaning of tanks. Tanks are not disinfected and not properly covered, hence stored water is prone to pollution and mosquito breeding. Supply is better but problems of small storage tanks and utility rationing limit continuity of supply.	Competition from communal boreholes with water of acceptable quality sold at TSh10 per 20-litre jerrycan.	20	1000/m³
Water sold from kiosk connection to DAWASA mains.	Good quality water in varying qualities. Payment on the spot or flat rate monthly.	Good quality potable water. Supply is dependent on utility rationing pattern; continuity of supply constrained by lack of storage tanks and water rationing.	Connected resellers in the neighbourhood with water storage tanks.	10 Price at source Price to end-user	500-1000/m³ 3500/m³ to 7500/m³

(Table 7.2. continued on next page)

Table 7.2.	Characteristics of SWEs *(continued)*				
Potable water operators	Type of service and area of operation in informal settlement	Relative quality of service	Competition for market	Price	
				TSh/20-litre jerrycan	TSh/m³
Connected resellers					
Tanker trucks	Water is sold wholesale by tankers (7–10m³) to affluent households located far away from informal settlements. Good quality water acceptable to consumers (households, industries, building sites, etc.). Sale price is fixed with some minor variations depending on size of tanker, distance, etc.	Good quality potable water that is acceptable to consumers.			Price at source 600–700/m³ Price to end-user 3000/m³
Communal borehole	Water is sold directly from taps at the borehole site. Borehole has electric pump. Potable water of acceptable quality supplied from storage tank. Price is fixed; payment on the spot. No extension of distribution pipe and kiosks to neighbourhood.	Good quality potable water that is acceptable to the consumers.	Competition from private borehole owners with large elevated water storage tanks to meet customer water needs and high supply pressure to reduce queuing time; standby electric generators to maintain continuous supply during power supply interruptions and extension of distribution system and kiosks to neighbourhood.	10	500/m³

(Table 7.2. continued on next page)

Table 7.2.	Characteristics of SWEs *(continued)*				
Potable water operators	Type of service and area of operation in informal settlement	Relative quality of service	Competition for market	Price	
				TSh/20-litre jerrycan	TSh/m³
Connected resellers					
Private boreholes	Water sold from kiosk(s) located at borehole site and from kiosks supplied by extension of a distribution pipe from storage tank. Good quality water, acceptable to consumers. Price is fixed but increases during power supply interruptions when standby generator is turned on. Water sold retail and wholesale.	Good quality potable water acceptable to consumers.	Competition from other private borehole owners with elevated large water storage tanks to meet customer water needs and high supply pressure to reduce water collecting time, standby electric generator to maintain continuous supply in the event of supply failure and distribution system extension and kiosks in neighbourhood.	20-30	1000/m³ to 1500/m³

Notes:
1. Utility connection holders in the informal settlements are changed a flat monthly bill of TSh12,000.
2. Utility applicable tariff for kiosks is TSh337/m³.

	Focus group	Group code
1.	Owners of private boreholes	A
2.	Street water vendors	B
3.	Community-managed boreholes	C

Table 7.3.	Constraints facing SWEs		
Constraints / weaknesses reported		**Group code**	**Problem group code**
1.	Our water is good but a bit saline. It is also not as a clear as the utility's (DAWASA), which is not saline.	A	4
2.	We wait in a queue in order to collect water.	B	5
3.	Most of the revenue collected is used to pay electricity bills.	C	2
4.	In a day, electric power consumed ranges between 15–20kW. The cost of power consumed in a day is higher than the revenue collected per day.	A	2
5.	Utility (DAWASA) water is available far away in Kibasila area.	B	8
6.	Pump installed is of smaller capacity compared to the volume (yield) of water that the borehole can safely provide.	C	5
7.	In cases where the borehole owner possesses electric appliances such as a refrigerator and electric iron box in his house the cost of electricity becomes very high.	A	2
8.	When there is power supply interruption, water is not available at the borehole sources because most of the borehole pumps are driven by electricity.	B	2
9.	Water from borehole has a salty taste.	C	4
10.	The water vending business is good but the major problem is high cost of power supply. In a month 100 units of power are consumed. Half of the monthly revenue collected is used to pay the electricity bill and the remaining half is used for the maintenance of the borehole.	A	2
11.	There is plenty of water in the boreholes but most of it is salty.	B	4
12.	Some customers claim the right to be given free water from a community-managed borehole since the borehole is a government property.	C	12
13.	Lack of funds to invest in water storage tank causes consumption of more units of power. With a water storage tank less power is used.	A	9

(Table 7.3. continued on next page)

Table 7.3. Constraints facing SWEs *(continued)*

Constraints / weaknesses reported		Group code	Problem group code
14.	We do not have reliable written contracts with our customers.	B	1
15.	Some customers collect water from the borehole on credit but do not settle their bills when due.	C	3
16.	My problem is that I have small water storage tanks which cause me to switch on the pump (power) more frequently.	A	9
17.	Some of the customers refuse to pay for the water consumed.	B	3
18.	There are internal disputes among the community members responsible for managing the water supply system.	C	13
19.	There is no standby power generator; so during public power supply interruptions water supply business stops because of the lack of power to run the pump.	A	9
20.	We have disputes with customers (monthly bills) who have failed to pay the outstanding bill.	B	3
21.	Some customers do not like to wait in a queue and therefore ask for priority service based on several pretexts, e.g. hurrying to a funeral of a close relative or to a hospital to see a very sick relative, etc.	C	3
22.	Although we are delivering a water supply service, the supply itself is not enough. In between 9am and 12 noon the supply usually goes down.	A	5
23.	When there is a water supply interruption we are forced to collect water from far away sources.	B	8
24.	The community-managed kiosks are facing increasing competition from private individuals who own boreholes equipped with large capacity pumps, storage tanks and standby electric generators.	C	2
26.	Some of the customers are quarrelsome; some pour out the water already collected claiming that it is not clean.	A	3
27.	There are no written contracts with our customers. Therefore 'we are exploited'.	B	1
28.	There is no association which unites community-managed kiosks in order to safeguard their business interests.	C	10

(Table 7.3. continued on next page)

Table 7.3. Constraints facing SWEs *(continued)*		
Constraints / weaknesses reported	**Group code**	**Problem group code**
29. Some customers use a lot of water at the source for cleaning their buckets.	A	3
30. Quarrels arise at the water collection sources because some people decide not to wait in a queue. Sometimes the strong ones force their way to collect water first.	B	3
31. There is no forum for discussion of issues/problems related to community-managed boreholes.	C	10
32. Some customers decide to put their buckets in the queue for collecting water and walk away for some other activities on the understanding that the buckets will retain the customer's positions in the queue on their return, something which often causes disputes among the customers in the long queue and the borehole owner.	A	3
33. Continuous pushing of carts causes strains on the ribs and chest.	B	6
34. Many customers deliberately come to the source with a number of small non-standard containers in order to collect free water. The 20-litre and 10-litre bucket/jerrycan are the locally acceptable units of measure in the water vending business.	A	3
35. During the dry season there is a shortage of water.	B	5
36. Some customers used to pay their bills on a monthly basis. A flat rate was charged for unlimited water use. The monthly billing practice was stopped on discovering that some unfaithful customers used to collect water for themselves and for their neighbours as well.	A	3
37. The street water vending market is going down. When I started water vending in 1987 there was more business and it paid better.	B	7
38. In Temeke district there has been an increase in conmen claiming to be shallow well construction experts.	A	11
39. Our customers are selective in the type of water source they want. Some customers prefer DAWASA water while others prefer water from boreholes.	B	4

Notes:
Group code A = Focus group: Owners of private boreholes
Group code B = Focus group: Street water vendors
Group code C = Focus group: Community-managed boreholes

Problem group code	Problem group category	Score	Ranking
Table 7.4.	SWEs' perspectives about their own constraints		
1	Lack of formal written contracts	2	6 =
2	Power supply interruptions and high cost of electricity	6	2
3	Poor relations with customers	10	1
4	Poor water quality	4	3 =
5	Inadequate water quantity	4	3 =
6	Occupational health hazards characterized by strains on chest, ribs, etc.	1	9 =
7	Competition in the water market	1	9 =
8	Water accessibility problems	2	6 =
9	Inadequate capital for investment	3	5
10	Lack of umbrella association for small water enterprises	2	6 =
11	Poor/wrong advice on appropriate well technology	1	9 =
12	People's perception of water as a free commodity	1	9 =
13	Lack of efficient management	1	9 =

1. The issue of the poor water quality delivered by SWEs, especially street water vendors, has been raised by both the SWEs and consumers interviewed (see Section 8.2). The SWEs agree that poor water quality is a constraint to their commercial business interests, whereas the consumers are suspicious about the quality of vended water and see it as a potential health threat. It is also a loss of their meagre income if they buy water and cannot distinguish with their eyes between water collected from safe sources and from poor sources.

Problems of poor water quality and accessibility/inadequate quantities in the informal settlements force the pushcart vendors to fetch water from utility piped sources far away and to sell the water at a higher price to the low-income households. The higher cost charged compensates for the long-distance transportation costs. Walking and pushing a cart over long distances in search of the good quality water demanded by customers and selling the water at a higher price is not a motivation to the vendors because the practice causes health hazards (strains on ribs and chest).

2. The vendors would prefer to have a piped water source nearby for their business. A nearby utility source would also be advantageous to the consumer in terms of quality and cost.

3. The problems of poor water quality and high prices charged by vendors could be alleviated by extending utility distribution pipe to the unserved or inadequately served informal settlements and installing utility kiosks that will provide good quality water at controlled and affordable prices (see also 'SWEs weaknesses and opportunities' in Chapter 10 – Consensus Building).

SWOT analysis of SWEs

The responses obtained from individual interviews and focus group discussions held in the SWE study areas (Sandali, Yombo Vituka , Mtoni, Azimio, Mtoni and Buguruni wards) were analysed using a SWOT analysis for each group of SWE (street water vendors, communal water kiosks, communal and private borehole water supply systems). The strengths, weaknesses, opportunities and threats facing the different SWEs are summarized below.

Table 7.5. Street water vending

Strengths	Weaknesses	Opportunities	Threats
Availability of water of good quality from utility source/service connection holders Provision of water services to match consumer needs and financial ability	Scarcity of water during dry season Physically difficult operation Low financial return Water supplied is of questionable quality Lack of personal cleanliness/water Carrying containers Lack of written contracts with customer on monthly bill	Water shortage Employment/income Form network/ association Inefficiency/lack of capacity and resources in water utilities	Occupational health hazards (illness/ weak health – e.g. chest pains due to strenuous work, etc.) Competition from private and communal borehole and kiosks and younger street vendors Availability of alternative water sources Distance to source Alternative/favourable source of income

Table 7.6. Communal water kiosks (connected to utility system)			
Strengths	**Weaknesses**	**Opportunities**	**Threats**
Affordable to communities Serve more people Source of water of good quality for unconnected population O&M costs are minimum Well-established management procedures Communal water supply options supported by revised water policy	Lack of continuous supply from utility network Lack of water storage facility to balance consumer demand Water wastage (kiosk not metered and repaired promptly) Low sales during rainy season Low price which does not cover costs Poor recording and reconciliation of water sales and revenue on daily basis Failure by some customers to settle their monthly bills when due Lack of transparency and poor accountability of revenue collected Voluntary labour for operating kiosk and collecting revenue is provided by some of the water committee members Environmental degradation resulting from poor drainage/water disposal at supply point	Ability to serve bigger population with less cost Community delegation of operation of kiosk to local operator under contract to enhance efficiency in service delivery Capacity building of management through training	Increase in household connections Household resellers of utility water with storage tanks installed in neighbourhood of communal water kiosk Competition from private boreholes especially those with distribution network Rainwater harvesting

Communal Water Kiosks

Lessons

- System will work better when the kiosk is metered and installed with water balancing tank.
- Use of voluntary managers is not geared to efficient management of the water services.
- Tariff should be affordable and recover operation and maintenance costs.
- Communities should refrain from direct operation of kiosks in order to engender efficient delivery of services.
- There is room for utility/community/private operator i.e. SWEs to work as partners in efficient service delivery for mutual benefit.

Issues

1. Institutional

- Communal kiosks to be run under contract by private operator(s) as agents of communities

2. Financial

- Economic and affordable water charges should be established by the community to ensure recovery of costs and financial sustainability.
- Prompt/pre-payment method is recommended to safeguard consumers of the kiosk service against disconnection (customers to make payment every time water is collected and adopt shorter payment period(s) for monthly billed customers to match financial capability of customers).

3. Legal

- There should be a valid contract between the community and kiosk operator.
- There should be a written contract with monthly billed customers.
- In the event of disconnection consideration should be given by water utility to the customers of the kiosk service.

4. Management

- Voluntary management should be discouraged; paid kiosk operators supervised by management should be employed under contract with communities.

5.   Location of kiosks

* Future location of suitable site(s) for communal kiosks should be agreed by utility in consultation with communities in the un-served informal settlements taking into consideration population density and other technical factors.

Table 7.7. Community-managed boreholes			
Strengths	**Weaknesses**	**Opportunities**	**Threats**
Well-written community water supply management procedures Community water supply management practice supported by water policy Community-based approaches recognized and supported by utilities	Inefficiencies related to voluntary labour provided by some of water committee members for operating the system and revenue collection Inadequate transparency and accountability for revenue collected Political interference in the management of services Weak financial and general management Failure of customers to pay their monthly bills when due Low sales during rainy season Lack of timely response to operational/ maintenance problems High cost of electricity compared to income Lack of standby power generator to mitigate against public power supply interruptions and failures Lack of umbrella association for community-managed water supply systems Poor drainage at water collection points	Enhancement of capacity building through training and empowerment Separation of management from operations to enhance efficiency Delegation of water supply management to a private operator Improvement/ Increase of capacity and efficiency of existing facilities	Competition from private borehole owners with standby electric power generators, water balancing storage tanks and water distribution network Private and communal boreholes with water that is not saline Extension of utility network to the community borehole supply area

Recommendation

Install communal kiosks with water balancing storage tanks at suitable locations in informal settlements that will be managed by small local operators under contract.

Community-managed systems

Lessons

- The community-managed systems are not financially sustainable.
- The setting of water charges should consider consumer affordability and financial sustainability of the services.
- The community-managed water supply systems will work better in the absence of political interference in the management of the water services.
- The use of voluntary labour from among water committee members to operate the water supply system and collect revenue is not conducive to efficient, transparent and effective management of the water supply services.
- Community management of the borehole water supply system should refrain from direct operation of the system.
- There is a potential opportunity for the community to work with small private operators under a contract in order to deliver services more efficiently and in a financially sustainable manner for the mutual benefit of the consumers, the community and the private operator.

Further details concerning issues and recommendations emanating from the study are given below.

Issues

1. Institutional

- The water supply should be run under contract by a small local private operator as agent of the community.

2. Financial

- Review tariff to ensure efficient cost recovery and financial sustainability.
- Encourage on the spot payment every time consumers collect water.
- For the current monthly billed customers a shorter billing period should be considered to match consumers' financial capability.
- Meter all water that is supplied and sold at the supply point in order to monitor quantity of water supplied and revenue collected.
- Maintain daily record of sales and revenue.

- Reconcile total water sales and revenue collected on a daily basis.
- Revenue collected should be deposited in a bank account operated by the community.
- Build capacity of management staff through tailor-made financial and general management training.
- Increase customer base by extending distribution system and kiosks to unserved neighbourhoods. (This activity should consider available yield from borehole, population, local water demand, storage capacity and hydraulic design characteristics, etc.)
- Provide access to finance and credit facilities.

3. Legal

- There should be a valid contract (lease) between the community and the small local operator. A one-year contract renewable subject to approval by community is proposed.

4. Management

- Voluntary managers should be discouraged. Instead managers should be paid an amount to be decided by the community.
- Shared management responsibilities are proposed. In this regard the community, through its water committee, should be responsible for water production, any network extension, major system repairs (electric pumping system, storage tanks and distribution), and supervision of the operator. The operator should be responsible for water production, distribution, routine maintenance, sale of water at price set by community, employment of water (kiosk) attendants, security guards, and any applicable municipal taxes on the business.
- Agreement should be reached on the percentage of revenue to be retained by operator (to ensure continuity of operation and maintenance activities plus some profit margin) and the rest to be remitted to the community for capital investment and major repairs, etc.

Recommendation

- Community should subcontract (lease) community-managed water supply services to a competitively selected small local operator under a one-year contract renewable on successful performance in the previous year's contract.

Table 7.8. Private borehole water supply systems

Strengths	Weaknesses	Opportunities	Threats
Private sector participation in water sector supported by revised water policy and existing legislation Assessment and recognition of small independent providers emphasized by revised water policy Private borehole water services are filling water supply gap left by utilities in unserved low-income informal settlements	Unaware of existing water policy and legislation on groundwater abstraction and use Lack of umbrella association of private borehole water suppliers/ SWEs Low sales during rainy season Formal recognition by utilities is lacking Partnership/formal interaction with utilities is non existent Lack of entrepreneurship knowledge and skills Lack of formal contracts with monthly billed customers Lack of water supply system records Poor or no drainage system at supply points Some boreholes are prone to pollution because they are located close to household pit latrines Frequent power supply interruptions affecting continuous supply of water Lack of standby power supply generators High cost of electricity compared to income Lack of access to credit facilities Not recognized by law yet	Legitimization of small independent water providers in line with the provisions of the revised water policy Recognition by utilities Access to finance and credit facilities Mutual working partnership with utilities	Extension of utility piped water supply to the private borehole supply area Frequent power supply interruptions and high cost of electricity Competition from fellow private borehole owners with standby power generators, large storage tanks and water distribution system

Private Boreholes

Lessons

1. Increased water shortages in the informal settlements led to the development of private boreholes which have helped to reduce the shortages in the study area during the five years.
2. Location and drilling of some of the boreholes studied have not adhered to the existing groundwater development procedures and regulations, partly due to lack of public education on the matter and lack of enforcement of existing regulations concerning groundwater abstraction and management. Only one private borehole owner in the study area (in Yombo Vituka Ward) had obtained a Water Right. The rest claimed to be unaware of the regulatory requirement.
3. Compared to the other SWEs, private borehole water supply systems are more efficiently managed and therefore deliver services in a more sustainable manner.
4. Formal recognition of the private borehole water supply systems by utilities is lacking. In addition umbrella associations for private borehole owners to help promote and protect their business interests is also lacking. Efforts to improve SWE services should therefore address these problem areas.

Issues

1. Institutional

- Formal recognition by utilities will help in the formation of associations of private borehole owners. The association, in collaboration with utilities, will enable SWEs to understand the procedures and regulations for groundwater abstraction and management, type of technology to be used, hygiene education, water supply, water pricing, etc.
- Capacity building to be facilitated through NGOs and utilities will help to develop the entrepreneurial knowledge and skills of the borehole owners and their operators/attendants.

2. Financial

- Provide tailor-made financial and general management training for private borehole owners and their workers. Training can be provided by NGOs, utilities and consultants.
- The financial issues raised and suggestions made under the community-managed boreholes are equally relevant to private borehole water supply systems.

3. Legal

- Private borehole enterprises need legal recognition to enhance their development. Private borehole owners are presently operating informally. They do not have a legal status but the revised water policy recognizes them. Revision of existing water laws to accommodate the provisions of the water policy is expected to legitimize and facilitate the further development of private borehole water supply systems and SWEs in general.
- Written contracts between private borehole owners and monthly billed consumers are necessary.

Recommendation
- Utilities should formally recognize private borehole water systems, which are efficient and deliver services in a sustainable way under private management.

Chapter 8

Consumers' Perspectives on SWEs

8.1 Methodology

The study team interviewed 20 key consumers representing various customer segments in Sandali Ward. Focus group meetings were also held with five consumer groups, each consisting of about 8 to 12 people, in order to determine the available service options and customer views on aspects such as technology, price and water quality. The focus group meetings helped to sharpen and cross-check individual attitudes of consumers to SWEs.

8.2 Consumer perspectives on SWEs

General

The individual and focus group consumers interviewed included: women, men, schoolchildren, the poorest as defined by the community concerned, people with disabilities, food vendors, local brewers, people who wash clothes, and owners of restaurants and guesthouses.

The consumers interviewed had a common opinion that the SWEs (street water vendors, private borehole owners, community-managed boreholes, utility kiosks managed by communities, neighbours with utility private water connection /yard tap) operating in the Sandali Ward were doing an indispensable service to the people living in the settlement and at the same time were creating employment for themselves.

In particular they commended the private individuals who have increased the number of water supply boreholes in the settlement since 2000. Some of the respondents described the private borehole owners as 'Wakombozi wa maji', i.e. 'saviours of water supply'.

The drought of 1997, which affected many parts of the country, caused very low water flows in the Ruvu River, which supplies most of the water to the city. The ensuing water crisis caused the government, in collaboration with external donors, to embark on an emergency programme to drill over 200 boreholes in the Dar es Salaam city area. Private individuals also drilled their own boreholes using the services of the Drilling and Dam Construction Agency (DDCA) of the Ministry of Water or private drillers. The borehole owners started selling water to the unserved neighbourhoods in order to recover investment and operation and maintenance costs. Consultations with local leaders during the study revealed that political leaders and other leaders in and outside Sandali Ward have been encouraging private individuals to drill boreholes to supply water to the unserved settlements.

The people interviewed complained about the 'high' average purchase price of TSh20 charged for a 20-litre jerrycan of water at most of the protected alternative sources and the 'high' average sale price of TSh100–150 charged by street water vendors for the same amount of water when delivered to the household. The price of TSh20 at the source is widely applied in the city although there is no mechanism or forum to establish or regulate the price charged by water vendors. With regard to the perceived higher sale price charged by the vendors, the people and especially the women interviewed said they had the cheaper alternative of walking to a perceived safe source of water to purchase water at TSh20 for a 20-litre jerrycan of water.

The people who cannot afford the above water supply charges resort to the nearby unsafe traditional river water source (Yombo River) and hand-dug wells in the riverbed, especially for water for washing and cleaning purposes.

Service options
The range of sources or supply options available in the settlement include:

- river
- hand-dug wells
- rainwater harvesting
- private shallow wells with handpump
- communal water kiosk
- neighbours piped connection
- communal water boreholes
- street water vending
- private water boreholes

The individual consumers and the consumer focus groups interviewed concerning the above service options had a range of views revolving around a number of convenience factors including: quantity and quality of water available from a specific source; distance of the source from the household; time to collect water; reliability of the source of supply; and the relative cost of water at the source and when transported to the household.

River
The Yombo River is the available surface water source for the settlement. The river water is dark and smells foul due to both wastewater discharges from the Nyerere Road industrial area located upstream as well as household wastewater discharged directly into the river.

The interviews conducted with households reveal that the river water is used mainly for washing clothes and household cooking/kitchen utensils, as well as for bathing and sometimes for brewing beer. During the study period children were seen playing and bathing in the polluted river.

The average walking distance to the river is about 0.5 km.

Water quality
The respondents said cholera and other diseases like diarrhoea and dysentery are endemic in the area and attributed the diseases to unsafe water supply sources including the Yombo River. They also said that the Yombo River was the source of bilharzia in the settlement in the past but that the disease has now long disappeared.

Sandali and other settlements adjoining the Yombo River are frequently affected by cholera outbreaks. Although the people interviewed attributed cholera to unsafe water it should be noted that poor sanitation characterized by traditional pit latrines which are widely used in the settlement in combination with poor health/hygiene practices in the settlements also contribute to the frequent cholera outbreaks.

The quality of the river water is generally unfit for any household use.

Cost of water
The river is not a preferred source of water for household use by most of the people interviewed. However, people who cannot afford higher quality water for bathing, washing and cleaning resort to the unsafe traditional river water source.

Hand-dug wells
Hand-dug traditional shallow wells are located in the riverbed of the Yombo. The characteristics of the water from the shallow wells and the perceptions of the people interviewed concerning these wells are similar to those given for the Yombo River source above.

Technology in use
The wells are dug in the riverbed sand by the residents using normal hand tools like hoes and spades. Empty 200-litre steel tanks perforated with holes in the lower half are sunk into a pit dug in the riverbed sand leaving the upper part (say 30 cm) protruding above the sand bed. Water from the surrounding sand bed filters into the tank through the perforations ready for collection by the residents.

Water quality
The water collected in the wells is dark and smells foul because of the industrial and household wastewater discharged into the river. The water is generally unfit for any household use.

Cost of water
The residents who cannot afford the more expensive alternative sources walk to the unsafe traditional well sources to collect free water for bathing, washing, cleaning and sometimes for making local beer.

Rainwater harvesting
This water supply option is used by the people in the settlement who collect water from their house's corrugated iron roof and store it in household containers during the rainy season. The bulk of the rain falls between March and May, but continued showers throughout the year are common. The total rainfall per year ranges between 1,000 and 1,400 mm. The small capacity storage containers (small tanks and buckets) usually available in the households limit the amount of rainwater that can be harvested and stored for use over a long period of time. The alternative sources including boreholes, protected shallow wells and the water utility pipes also have increased supply during the rainy season.

Water quality
Although rainwater collects dust from the roof catchment, it is not saline and therefore perceived by people to be of good quality.

Cost of water
Rainwater is free to households.

Additional costs for interested consumers (especially primary schools and hospitals where rainwater harvesting is on the increase in other areas outside Sandali) would be required to provide gutters and storage tanks which would also require space for their construction.

Private shallow wells with handpump

There are few private shallow wells with handpumps in the area. The shallow wells visited were in Mamboleo B Sub-ward, which also had private boreholes nearby. The people said it takes longer to queue at a shallow well in order to collect the amount of water desired and the situation becomes worse during the dry season when the groundwater table falls.

Technology in use

The shallow wells with handpumps are operated manually. These wells, unlike the private boreholes, communal boreholes and kiosks, and the neighbour's connection, are not affected by power supply fluctuations.

Water quality

The people interviewed said that the quality of shallow well water was questionable because they were located in household premises and therefore were prone to pollution as a result of possible infiltration of household pit latrine wastewater.

Cost of water

Water from shallow wells is sold at TSh10–20 per 20-litre jerrycan.

Communal water kiosk

In the past, DAWASA and its predecessor, NUWA, provided water from the distribution mains at standpipes located around the city. Many of these standpipes were closed by DAWASA due to vandalism and disrepair caused by lack of ownership and operational management (supervision of standpipes, maintenance and revenue collection).

Dar es Salaam City Council used to pay for water supplied through these kiosks but later the payments stopped. A few of the standpipes are now being operated by communities who have opened an account with DAWASA. These private standpipe operators who sell water directly to people and water vendors are billed monthly by City Water Services on an assessed rate basis or on metered consumption.

Under the Dar es Salaam Water Supply and Sanitation Project, City Water Services will construct and equip 250 public water kiosks for use by urban residents who would not be in a position to acquire private water connections. In order to avoid a repeat of the previous experience the utility operator will use agents to manage and operate the kiosks in order to secure long-term sustainability of the facilities.

The Mtoni-Nkenge community water kiosk was visited during the study. The kiosk is managed by the community through a water committee elected by the community under the guidance of the Street Government. The committee consists of a chairman, secretary, treasurer and three committee members consisting of two women and a man. The community has been operating the kiosk over the last six years and has been able to pay the monthly water bills (TSh76,000 per month) over the entire period but has failed to maintain a cash deposit in their bank account. One member of the committee interviewed cited poor financial management as the underlying cause.

The potential customer base is high according to the committee members but the water supply service at the kiosk is inadequate in terms of availability and reliability.

Water supply at the kiosk comes from the nearby DAWASA Mtoni surface water plant through direct pumping into the distribution system. The supply is rationed by the utility and is usually available at the kiosk only between 7am and 10am. The kiosk water supply service deteriorated after 2002 following relocation of water pipelines on the nearby Kilwa road during the rehabilitation of the road.

This discontinuity in supply puts the community-managed kiosk at a competitive disadvantage with respect to nearby households with water connections which sell utility water to their neighbours. Such households have installed underground water storage tanks to mitigate against the effects of intermittent supply while the community-managed kiosk is not able to do so due to lack of funds. As a result the households are offering more reliable water retail services than the community-managed kiosks.

Two committee members (Secretary of the Water committee and one member of the committee) are responsible for revenue collection and they work on a voluntary basis. The community is also responsible for the operation and maintenance of the kiosk and for the security of the kiosk structure.

Water quality
The quality of water supplied at the kiosk is good and is preferred by the consumers.

Cost of water
The utility provides bulk supply service to the kiosk at TSh76,000 and the community retails it to consumers at TSh20 per 20-litre jerrycan or bucket. The kiosk is not metered.

Every household served by the kiosk is required to pay a flat rate of TSh1000/ per month and is allowed to collect any amount of water over the whole month.

Payment for the water is made every time water is collected or at the end of the month. Those outside the community are unable to collect water from the kiosk.

Neighbour's piped connection
Supply from a neighbour's connection is a water supply option used in a small area of the study settlement in Mwembeladu and Sandali Sub-wards (Mtaa) where the coverage of the utility network is inadequate and the utility water supply service is characterized by low water pressure and an irregular and unreliable supply.

The supply source (neighbour's pipe) is usually not metered, has water which tastes good, and has low pressure. Supply is available for only two or three hours a day two or three days a week (inconvenient supply). The supply is therefore unreliable, although the return travel time is less than five minutes.

Technology in use
Some owners of piped connections have installed underground water tanks to mitigate against the effects of the intermittent utility water supply and in so doing ensure a more reliable supply to the customers.

The underground water tanks are about 1.5 m long, 1 m wide and 2 m deep. They are made of concrete blocks and the top is usually covered with a light corrugated iron lid.

The capacity of the tanks is also relatively small compared to the water storage capacity needs of the consumers.

Water is collected from the tank using small containers with long handles or ropes. The area surrounding the storage tank lacks drainage.

Consumers prefer this service option for providing small amounts of good tasting water for drinking purposes.

In order to save time, consumers often leave their water containers (buckets) in a queue in the neighbour's premises to be filled and picked up later when the supply comes on.

Water quality
The water supplied is from the utility network. The consumers interviewed complained that although the tanks stored utility water which is superior in quality, the tanks were not cleaned regularly, which led to growth of green algae on the tank walls and made them a breeding ground for mosquito larvae.

Cost of water

The owner of the un-metered water connection pays a monthly flat rate fee of TSh12,000 to City Water Services.

The owner of the water connection retails to consumers at TSh20 per 20-litre jerrycan which is the prevailing rate in the study settlement and in many parts of the city. Consumers pay every time they collect water from the source.

Communal water boreholes

Water from boreholes has been used extensively in the city for many years. Prior to the 1997 water supply crisis caused by drought, there were many registered private boreholes supplying mainly industrial or commercial premises, most of which are still in use.

Under an emergency borehole drilling programme, 217 boreholes and tube wells were drilled, of which 193 are considered to be of adequate quality and quantity.

Of the 193 good boreholes, 31 are operated by DAWASA, 32 by institutions, and 55 by communities.

Water from the boreholes is supplied through taps located in the vicinity of the boreholes. All of these boreholes are under the ownership of DAWASA, and for those operated by communities DAWASA has issued Certificates of Handover which specify that the assets remain with DAWASA. Most of the community-operated boreholes have already been handed over by DAWASA.

In addition, under the World Bank-financed Urban Sector Rehabilitation Project (USRP), 46 boreholes were drilled in 1999 out of which 34 were successful. Seventeen of these boreholes with high yields (greater than 5 m^3/hr) are connected directly to the existing distribution system and are operated by the City Water Services. The remaining seventeen are managed by the communities. Water is supplied through metered standpipes.

Consumers' perception is that the community-managed boreholes have adequate water to meet consumers' demands at the water source. Long queues at the water source are common but the availability of supply is more assured in all seasons although during the dry season (October to January) the groundwater table drops slightly. Water supply is reliable if there is no public power supply interruption or mechanical failure and large enough storage tanks to maintain adequate water storage to meet water needs of consumers. Community-managed boreholes take longer to be repaired after mechanical breakdown because of internal consultations within the water committees before a decision is made and funds are made available for the needed repair. The return travel time is 15 minutes to 2 hours.

Water quality
The quality of the water supplied is generally acceptable to the consumers.

The borehole water is generally of acceptable quality and there is no water treatment or chlorination carried out. DAWASA monitors the quality of borehole water.

Cost of water
The price of water at communal water boreholes, just like in the other supply options, is not regulated by the utility. Water at the communal boreholes is sold at TSh10 per 20-litre jerrycan.

Street water vending
Street water vending using pushcarts is carried out widely in Sandali ward and in many parts of the city that are inadequately served (or not served at all) by the existing utility network. In the study area the vendors purchase water from owners of private boreholes, community-managed boreholes and kiosks, and private water connections located in areas with better utility services. They then transport it on pushcarts for sale in areas without water services.

Technology in use
Locally manufactured pushcarts (costing about TSh30,000–36,000) are used. The carts carry 6 to 10 20-litre jerrycans. (The cart that holds six jerry cans is preferred by many vendors.)

Water quality
The water delivered by water vendors is mainly used for drinking purposes and is perceived by consumers to be collected from safe and clean sources. However there is always an element of doubt on the quality of water supplied by pushcart vendors because the consumers cannot ascertain if the water is collected from a safe source.

Cost of water
According to consumers, the vendors purchase water at TSh20 per 20-litre jerrycan at the water source and sell it at TSh100–150.

Generally a household purchases one to two jerrycans of drinking water per day from pushcart vendors. Additional water for household use is obtained from other supply options, usually at a lower cost.

Private water boreholes

Private individuals and institutions have drilled their boreholes in Sandali and in many other wards in Dar es Salaam. These boreholes are used to supply water for their own households/institutions and for sale to other people in the settlements. In the Sandali ward drilling of boreholes by private individuals increased effectively from 2000.

Technology

According to the borehole owners, construction of deep boreholes requires an average investment cost[4] of TSh3-5 million to drill to a depth of 40 to 70 metres and install piping, pump and power supply, PVC storage tank, etc). The boreholes have immensely improved the water supply situation in the ward. They are equipped with submersible electric pumps and are able to deliver continuous supply over 24 hours provided there is no power supply interruption. (Monthly average cost of power supply ranges between TSh50,000–70,000, labour is usually provided by family members.)

Many of the private borehole owners have adequate water storage tanks to balance consumer consumption and a few of them own standby generators to ensure continuous (more reliable and accessible) supply during periods of public power supply interruptions which are common in the area. According to consumers, private borehole owners who do not own a generator and storage tanks of adequate capacity fail to maintain continuous supply.

Water quality

The water from many of these boreholes is salty but the salinity content is generally within tolerable limits and acceptable to consumers. According to them the water from these boreholes can be used for all household purposes.

Most consumers expressed strong views against private boreholes located in the close vicinity of household pit latrines. They said the human waste from the latrines would infiltrate into the boreholes and pollute the supply. They recommended future proper siting of boreholes in the settlement and that the borehole owners should continuously treat and disinfect the supply with the necessary water treatment chemicals and not according to the current practice of doing so only during cholera outbreaks.

In normal practice, the efficient management and monitoring of groundwater abstraction requires an institutional mechanism to continuously monitor the quantity and quality aspects of groundwater in an integrated way. There was no such mechanism in the study settlement.

Environmental considerations

The consumers noted that the areas surrounding the boreholes were characterized by pools of spilled water resulting from cleaning the women's buckets. The bad drainage at the water collection points made it difficult for the women to collect water. Such pools were also good breeding places for mosquitoes. The consumers recommended improving drainage at all the wells.

Cost of water

The consumers interviewed were willing to pay for services at the rate of TSh20–30 per 20-litre jerrycan of water. The higher rate of TSh30 is charged during power supply interruptions when the owner turns on a standby electric generator.

8.3   Summary of consumers' perspectives and recommendations

During the individual interviews and focus group discussions consumers were asked to give their opinion about and recommendations for SWEs and other consumers. The consumers perspectives and recommendations are summarized below.

Consumers' perspectives on some SWEs

The consumers interviewed gave the following information:

Private borehole owners

- Were providing water service to the community
- Had created employment for themselves
- Saved the community from water supply shortage problem

Street water vendors

- Have created employment for themselves
- Are helping the community to fetch water from distant sources
- Are providing an important service to the community

Some of the consumers were satisfied with the water supplied by the street water vendors who got their water from the DAWASA network, but were unhappy about the few water vendors perceived to collect and sell water from pools of water. They noted with concern that it was difficult for consumers to distinguish the source.

Other consumers felt that some street water vendors are not clean, wear dirty clothes, and use dirty jerrycans, therefore the water supplied by them was also not clean.

Consumers' recommendations to improve SWEs' services

Private borehole owners

- Should keep environment surrounding water sources clean and well drained
- Should disinfect borehole water before supplying it to consumers
- Should undergo training on borehole water supply management
- Pricing (and increasing price) of water should be based on actual operation and maintenance costs
- Number of boreholes should be increased in order to reduce the price of water and waiting time at the water sources
- Government should carry out hydrogeological investigations in the settlement in order to drill more boreholes

Street water vendors

- Should clean their clothes, jerrycans and their bodies
- Should not increase costs unnecessarily
- Should fetch water from safe and clean DAWASA sources and private or communal boreholes

Consumers' recommendations to water users

- Water for drinking should be boiled
- If the water is not boiled, consumers should use chemicals to disinfect the water
- Water should be used efficiently
- Consumers should collaborate with borehole owners in matters related to water supply

Observations

- Consumers see the SWEs as playing a valuable role in the provision of water supply services to unserved households, a role which the utilities and government have not yet managed to fulfil.
- Although consumers have cited some problems related to SWEs services, the concerns raised can be partly attributed to SWEs' ignorance of water supply technology and associated regulations and procedures, as well as health and hygiene education issues which could be addressed in order to improve SWEs services.

- Notwithstanding the concerns raised by consumers against SWEs, they will most likely continue to be of even greater importance in terms of local service provision as long as utility services continue to remain unavailable in the low-income settlements.
- The people in the low-income informal settlements (70–75 per cent of the city's population) are the potential majority future customers of the utility. Although the utilities have previously delivered services to relatively few areas, and they are working on projects or initiating plans to deliver more services to these unserved areas, at the moment consumers see the utilities as the cause of their water supply problems. They said that for a long time the utilities themselves have not managed to carry out their mandated roles in the informal settlements.
- Communities and SWEs alike are unaware of the provisions in their favour which are included in the revised national water policy, as well as in planned utility water supply strategies for the unserved informal settlements.
- For the utility (City Water Services) to cement its relationship with its majority future customers in the informal settlements, there is a need for the utility to initiate interactions and partnership between itself and SWEs who have been delivering water services to the settlements. Logistically, the SWEs live in the community and are familiar with and closer to the people, and perhaps better able to address their community's water supply needs to suit their cash flows, etc. Logistical costs are also lower for SWEs. The new partnerships could come about through utility kiosks which would to be operated contractually by SWEs. This relationship, which is expected to be of benefit to everyone – the utility, SWEs, and consumers – will avert possible future collusion of SWEs and/or consumers in sabotaging or vandalizing utility infrastructure and services.

---

4.   Cost data obtained from SWEs' (borehole owners) focus group discussions.

Chapter 9

Utility Perspectives on SWEs

9.1 Methodology

The study team conducted in-depth interviews with key informants from utilities (DAWASA, City Water Services, City Council and Temeke Municipality), Ministry of Water and Livestock Development, NGOs (Plan International, Equal Opportunities Trust Fund), and academics (University of Dar es Salaam and University College of Lands and Architectural Studies). The interviews were meant to collect the attitudes of utilities and organizations toward SWEs in order to explore options for improvement. The problems facing SWEs as identified by the utilities, and the utility suggestions for improving SWEs' services, are presented below, in Section 9.2.

9.2 Official perspectives on SWEs

Problems facing SWEs

1. Groundwater abstraction rights are not obtained from the Ministry of Water and Livestock Development by private borehole owners. They are ignorant of this requirement (PI, DAWASA).
2. Provision of water by SWEs is not a good solution because it is difficult to control water quality, especially for street vendors. The vendors only interest is getting money, so sometimes they lie that they are providing piped water; the only way to exercise control is to install many metered DAWASA kiosks (TMC).
3. If City Water Services and DAWASA can expand their water services to reach everyone with sufficient quantity and potable quality SWEs would die away (UCLAS).
4. Some of the private wells have good quality water and others do not (TMC).
5. Water vending could be a permanent water supply solution provided enough resources were available, but funds, especially for the improvement and expansion of the water supply system, continue to be a problem (CC).

6. Street water vending and private wells are not a permanent solution. However government has not yet supplied water to the unserved areas. Once water reaches there the vendors will move out to the furthest places.

7. Water vendors fetch water from shallow wells and streams, but this water is not safe for human consumption (CWs).

8. Some religious groups do not follow the procedures for project preparation and do not contact the municipality for advice, which sometimes leads to problems, for example the Muslim Society dug a well in swamps (TMC).

9. We have no communication with street vendors and there is no formal interaction with them (TMC, DAWASA).

10. Water provided by vendors is of suspicious quality because of the existence of pit latrines and sewerage systems close to the groundwater sources used by the vendors. Discharges from these systems can pollute shallow wells and boreholes (UD).

11. Some community borehole water supply systems have experienced management problems (PI).

12. The problem is that water from some of the boreholes may not be safe because the boreholes are drilled close to pit latrines (EOTF, PI).

13. The quality of water they supply is suspect (UCLAS, DAWASA).

14. Shallow wells are generally unsafe sources, which contributes extensively to cholera epidemics, and this is compounded by people's poor hygiene habits (CC).

15. Other vendors are providing poor quality contaminated water that leads to cholera outbreaks. The Municipal Council therefore has to pay to treat the sick people (CC).

16. Prices differ and are sometimes hiked during water shortages. We ask the government to think about controlling vendors' quality and price. They have to be controlled (CWs).

17. I normally trust the quality of water from DAWASA since the water from wells can be contaminated by pit latrines (EOTF).

18. The management of community water utilities is difficult as they are dominated by conflicts of interests between street government and water committees: street leaders sometimes abuse their power. Sometimes committee members are taken to court as they do not deposit the revenue collected into the committee's bank A/C (TMC).

19. Provision of water by vendors is not a good solution at all, because shallow wells and deep wells can be contaminated through infiltration of pit latrine wastewater into the boreholes (CWs).

20. There are problems in financial management for community-managed projects financed by the municipality (PI).

21. Groundwater is a natural resource. Individuals and private organizations like hotels are taking water from the ground and believe that it is their water and they are not paying for it. They should know that they are taking Tanzania's natural resource, which is not a free commodity (CWs, DAWASA).

22. At present there are no regulations for water vendors (MoWLD, DAWASA).

23. There is a linkage between DAWASA and bowser (tanker trucks) owners but the owners charge high prices especially during water shortage periods (EOTF).

24. Water supplied by vendors is of suspicious quality, because its source may be unknown, and it may become contaminated during transportation from the source to the customer (UD).

25. There is no regulation for water vendors at the moment (UCLAS).

26. The water vendors are petty traders who have no legal status; they are not registered, have no licence and cannot be followed up in terms of adhering to standards and control. However the vendors know that if they sell unsafe water they are liable to punishment under the Food and Beverage Act (CC).

27. Private borehole owners are ignorant of the importance of geological features of the underlying rock/soil formations in relation to water quality; sometimes they drill their boreholes close to pit latrines (MoWLD).

28. Street vendors collect water from public water pipes. In this case the quality is higher and the price (and profit margin) are also higher (MoWLD).

29. We are not sure of the quality of the water they supply since we don't know where they fetch it from (EOTF).

30. Ministry does not encourage water vending since vendors are not knowledgeable about water quality and the relationship between water quality and the underlying geological formations. Groundwater technology is a problem for private borehole owners (MoWLD).

31. Selfishness is still a problem in Community Project Management (Financial Management) (PI).

32. Bowser (tanker trucks) owners sell water at a very high price (EOTF).

33. Means of transportation increases the cost of vended water and the quality of water goes down during handling and transportation; as a result the customers carry the burden (MoWLD).

34. Private borehole owners are required to treat their water before supply to consumers. This practice is mainly reinforced during cholera outbreaks (PI).

35. Only one tanker owner interacts with us but there are more than 100 tankers providing water to unserved people (CWs).

36. Tanker truck owners purchase cheap good-quality water for about TSh4,000 for 10,000 litres. But they sell it at about ten times the price (TSh40,000 to TSh50,000) for the same amount of water. They make huge profits and this is exploitation of the customers and therefore the government needs to take action on this (CWs).
37. SWEs do not have an umbrella association (PI).
38. SWEs are not recognized by the water utilities (PI).

Observations

It can be observed from the above summary of the list of problems facing SWEs, as perceived by government officials and water utility staff interviewed, that the constraints facing the latter in recognizing SWEs mainly relate to community health, laws and regulations, and price factors – in that order. These factors are characterized by:

• Poor/questionable water quality, which is a threat to the health of the community, and lack of price control for water delivered by SWEs, especially street water vendors.
• Uncontrolled borehole drilling and unregulated groundwater abstraction leads to inappropriate location of private boreholes (close to pit latrines, thus making the boreholes prone to pollution by pit latrine waste) contrary to groundwater abstraction regulations and management.

The remaining problems (lack of recognition of SWEs, interaction/partnership between utilities and SWEs, investment capital, and an SWE umbrella association) received fewer but a similar number of responses from the utilities and therefore have a similar ranking. These problems will nonetheless constitute major constraints to any efforts to developing SWEs as perceived by SWEs themselves (see below).

Comparison of perceptions

The following problems have been highlighted by both utilities and SWEs.

• Poor water quality
• Inadequate capital for investing in SWE activities
• Lack of umbrella association to promote and safeguard SWEs' business interests
• Lack of efficient management, especially for community borehole water supply systems

Table 9.1. Summary of problems facing SWEs		
Problem group category	**Score**	**Rank**
1. Lack of laws and regulations for SWEs	7	2
2. High price	6	3
3. Poor water quality	17	1
4. Water vending is a temporary business	2	5 =
5. Lack of capital	1	7 =
6. Mismanagement	4	4
7. Environmental degradation	2	5 =
8. Lack of recognition of SWEs	1	7 =
9. Lack of SWE umbrella association	1	7 =
10. Lack of interaction with water utilities	1	7 =

Contrast of perceptions

- Lack of recognition of SWEs is a problem that appears on the utilities' list of perceptions. This problem, however, does not appear on the list of problems cited by SWEs themselves, probably because SWEs at present have an assured market for water services in their localities.
- While utilities have cited the high prices charged by vendors as a problem, the SWEs have directed their concerns to people's perception of water as a free commodity.

Utility suggestions for improving SWEs

1. Our intention is to install DAWASA-financed water kiosks in the unserved low-income informal areas located in our supply area (CWs).
2. Women will be employed under contract as agents to sell water at controlled prices (TSh15 per 20-litre jerrycan). The agent should maintain cleanliness at the kiosk and pay the monthly bills promptly (CWs).
3. We know we do not have water supply networks in some of our supply areas. The SWEs do supply water in such areas (CWs).

4. We can control SWEs by providing water through kiosks and the SWEs could work with us by collecting water from our kiosks and selling it in areas where we are not operating (CWs).
5. City Water currently has one kiosk which delivers water to tanker trucks (CWs).
6. We are not happy to see people vending water. We want people to get water from kiosks at low cost and at a reasonable distance from their households (CWs).
7. City Water cannot meet the present water demand. As a result SWEs should be supported not banned (UCLAS).
8. SWEs should be supported by government to extend their services (UCLAS).
9. An association of SWEs should be encouraged (UCLAS).
10. SWEs should not be banned because doing so may lead to poor quality services because the SWEs may decide to work illegally (UCLAS).
11. SWEs need to be monitored and regulated (UCLAS).
12. SWEs should be assisted in getting credit facilities to enable them to expand their services (UCLAS).
13. Some areas in Dar es Salaam do not have a water supply network; other areas have a network that does not deliver water (UD).
14. SWEs can be regulated; we could go back to kiosks, which should be metered and operated by a private agent. Let them pay tax (UD).
15. Protect the sources used by SWEs from pollution (UD).
16. The mandated utility may not have the resources to extend the water supply system to the unserved areas at present. Such areas are currently served by other providers (SWEs). Extension of the water supply system to such areas could be postponed to a later period thus allowing time to raise needed funds for the expansion of the system (UD).
17. Some of the unserved people can get potable water from regulated kiosks which are metered and operated by the other providers, that is SWEs (UD).
18. Linkages between mandated utilities and SWEs are important because it is difficult for the utilities to connect every person to the water system. Not all customers can afford the cost of water connection (UD).
19. Water vendors should be regulated by provision of water through kiosks; shallow wells have water of suspicious quality, so they need to be protected from pollution and have their quality monitored. Boreholes offer safer water supply sources (UD).
20. SWEs should be trained on water quality (PI).
21. SWEs should have an umbrella association (PI).

22. Drilling of deep wells should be carried out according to the required specifications and regulations. Water rights should be sought by SWEs (borehole owners).
23. SWEs should be recognized (PI).
24. Water tankers should collect water from official utility points (DAWASA).

Observations

- The SWEs have been striving to bridge the supply gap left by the utilities in the informal settlements.
- Overall, the views expressed by the different key utility stakeholders and officials support the of recognition of SWEs provided controls are exercised on the quality of water supplied and the price charged.
- Most utility stakeholders and officials support installing utility kiosks to deliver water to households and street water vendors at a controlled price.
- Installation of utility kiosks will offer an opportunity for interaction/ partnership between SWEs and utilities for mutual benefit of and service to consumers.
- In the meantime, even if the utility will not recognize SWEs, the latter will continue to provide their services in light of the increasing supply–demand imbalance in the informal settlements.
- Although the supply gap is increasing, the government and the utilities do not have enough funds to extend the water supply system to reach the majority of the people living in the low-income settlements in the short term. This suggests that the SWEs' services will extend into the foreseeable feature, especially if water supply infrastructure and services are not extended to the informal settlements in the medium term.
- Under these circumstances and conditions it is important to find ways and means of improving SWEs' services for the benefit of customers, utility and SWEs themselves.
- Some officials have a perception that provision of water by SWEs might not be a good solution because it is difficult to control prices and water quality, especially for street water vendors. While there could be some problems in exercising the required controls, we need to realistically assess the feasible alternative options left with us in an atmosphere in which the government does not, for some reason, get the required capital investment to improve and extend water supply system to reach the majority of low-income settlements in the medium term. Obviously the use of SWE services in the informal settlements is one way of tapping local private sector financial resources and manpower into the water sector. However, for the SWEs to deliver acceptable services they need to be supported in terms of capacity building and finance.

- While the government is working on plans to extend services to the unserved informal settlements, it is worth taking advantage of improved SWE services. In the interim this approach would provide services to consumers and give sufficient time to government and utilities to plan and mobilize the needed resources for service expansion and improvement.

Chapter 10

Consensus Building

A workshop to review Phase 1 research findings and recommend Phase 2 pilot interventions was held on 20 April, 2004 at the Headquarters of the Vocational Education Training Authority (VETA) at Dar es Salaam. The workshop was attended by 32 participants including utility managers and several SWEs to compare the information collected, identify inconsistencies, draw conclusions on the research findings, and make recommendations for Phase 2 interventions.

The participants were grouped into three groups, with utility and SWE staff in each, to do SWOT analyses of the SWEs.

The following are the SWEs' strengths, weaknesses, opportunities and threats as identified by the three groups. The interventions proposed by the workshop are presented in Chapter 14.

Observations

The SWEs' strengths, weaknesses, opportunities and threats expressed by the workshop participants generally compare well and support the findings from the individual and group interviews and the discussions held with different key stakeholders including households, government officials and water utility staff and SWEs themselves. Notably, majority consensus was reached on the following aspects:

- SWEs are honoured and accepted in the local community because of their water supply services.
- The scarcity of utility water supply services is offering employment to water vendors and kiosk attendants in the settlements.
- Small/inadequate investment funds on the part of SWEs was cited as a constraint to the improvement of SWEs' water supply infrastructure and services.
- Due to inadequate utility water supply, SWEs have a guaranteed market for their services.
- The revised National Water Policy supports assessment and recognition of SWEs.

Table 10.1. SWOT analyses			
Strengths	**Strengths Group no.**	**Weaknesses**	**Weaknesses Group no.**
Are known and accepted in the community	1, 2	Poor business management (financial and project)	3
Have easy access to remote areas where the utility cannot reach – e.g. pushcarts vendors can deliver water to areas with impassable roads	3	Some SWEs are dishonest, e.g. they sell poor-quality water from pools to their customers	1
Know the location of the community	1	Lack of education (especially training on hygiene issues and business management)	2
Committed to providing services to the community, e.g. SWEs are ready to provide services whenever water is available even if it is very early in the morning	2	They are too profit-oriented, which leads to problems of selling poor quality water	3
Continuous supply of water (reliable supply)	3	Lack of small/capital Investment	1, 2, 3
Availability of labour	1	Lack of legal recognition	1
Provide services to unserved or underserved areas	2	Lack of water quality monitoring mechanism	2
Provide employment, e.g. kiosk attendant and vendors	1, 2, 3	Lack of credit facilities	3
Source of income	2	Shortage of safe water for supply	1
Builds strong relationship between customers and service providers	3	Lack of written contracts between customers and SWEs	2
Extra revenue (profit) could be used for other development projects in the community	3	Lack of security of their assets, e.g. theft/vandalism	3
They fill supply gap left by City Water/DAWASA		Lack of umbrella association for SWEs	1
Provide water according to user's financial capacity	3	Seasonal business, e.g. insecure market during rainy season	3
		Lack of laws and by-laws to regulate SWEs	3

(Table 10.1. continued on next page)

Opportunities	Opportunities Group no.	Threats	Threats Group no.
Guaranteed market due to inadequate supply of utility water	1, 2, 3	Financial management conflicts, especially for community-managed projects	3
Recognized by the National Water Policy	1, 2	Presence of City Water Service	1, 2, 3
Manpower (availability) for delivery of services	3	Increased planned areas with services	1
They have opportunities to access technical and financial assistance	2	Lack of guidelines for SWE activities	2
Availability of water sources	3	Unaware of existing laws and regulations and therefore fear them	
Community labour is available as a contribution to capital investment for community projects	3	Disorganized management, especially in the community-managed projects	3
		Competition among SWEs	1
		High investment and running costs	1
		Health, campaigns against unsafe water suppliers	1

Table 10.1. SWOT analyses (continued)

- Improvement of utility services in the SWEs' supply area was seen as a threat to SWE services.

Additional opportunities/incentives for improving SWEs' roles and services as cited by the participants included:

- Availability of manpower for SWEs' operations
- Availability of water sources
- Opportunities for access to local technical and financial assistance

According to the workshop participants, the threat to SWE services mentioned in the observation item about 'disorganized management' above would not exist if there were improved SWE services as well as a joint partnership between the utilities and the SWEs.

Chapter 11

Recommendations for Phase 2 Action Research

In coming up with the proposed pilot intervention for Phase 2 described below, the following factors/issues raised by consumers, SWEs, and utilities in the course of the study have been considered:

- Demand for utility piped water by consumers
- Reduced distance to source and reduced price
- Improved water quality
- Reliability of supply
- Health hazards on the part of vendors as a result of long-distance travel pushing carts

11.1 Study settlement (Sandali Ward)

The proposed beneficiary sub-wards are Mwembeladu and Sandali, with a population of 5,206 and 11,713 people respectively. These are among 31 sub-wards earmarked for water supply system upgrading through installation of water kiosks by City Water Services under the World Bank-financed Community Infrastructure Upgrading Programme (CIUP). According to preliminary consultations made with City Water Services in April 2004, nine kiosks will be constructed in Sandali Sub-ward and five in Mwembeladu, on the assumption that one kiosk will supply water to about 1,000–1,500 people (see Appendix 7). The distance between a kiosk and a household will depend on population density in the study settlement, among other factors. The number of pilot kiosk(s) will be determined soon.

It is proposed to carry out the pilot project in advance of the infrastructure upgrading programme and as such the capacity of the bulk supply pipe would have to be designed to cater for the final kiosk water supply requirements in the area. According to preliminary discussions with City Water Services, the implementation of the kiosk project under the CIUP is expected to begin next year but the actual start date is not yet set.

Most of the hardware part of the proposed intervention is likely to be financed under CIUP, while a large part of the software component is expected to be financed by the research project. It is proposed to firm up the financing plan and the implementation framework for the proposed intervention based on further discussions between WaterAid, City Water Services and the UK Study Team.

11.2 Installation of pilot utility kiosks in the study settlement

The proposed intervention includes:

- Extension of utility distribution pipe to the settlement to supply water through kiosk(s). In order to improve the reliability of supply through the kiosks it is also proposed to install a water storage tank at each kiosk.
- Involvement of the community (households and community leaders) in the appropriate location of the pilot kiosk. This approach is meant to ensure that the community participates in the planning process for the intervention.
- Empowerment of SWEs (private borehole owners, community-managed boreholes, and pushcart water vendors) to operate the kiosks on contractual agreement with the utilities. This approach will create opportunities for partnerships between SWEs and the utilities.
- Use of NGOs to involve communities in project planning, build capacity among SWEs, raise awareness on environmental and health issues among SWEs, and promote public awareness of SWE activities.

11.3 Tentative list of activities for Phase 2 (2004–06) intervention

A tentative list of proposed activities for Phase 2 and assignments of responsibilities to different parties is given below:

1. Hold meeting(s) (City Water, NGOs, SWEs, DAWASA, Municipal Council-Temeke) to discuss the proposed intervention and agree on activities to be carried out by each party. NGO to organize and coordinate discussions.
2. Hold discussions with beneficiary community concerning the proposed intervention. NGO to organize discussions.
3. Organize workshop (with stakeholders) to launch Phase 2 intervention. Utility and NGO to work together.
4. Discussion and agreement with community on appropriate locations of the kiosks. NGO and utility (City Water) to work together.
5. Survey and install distribution pipe to the settlement. Utility and NGO to work together.

6. Installation of kiosks – utility and NGO to work together.
7. Capacity building for kiosk operators (SWEs). NGO and utility will be responsible.
8. Creation of awareness on environmental and health issues among SWEs. NGO and utility will be responsible.
9. Commissioning of the installed utility kiosks. DAWASA, Utility and Temeke Municipality to work together.
10. Monitoring and evaluation of kiosk operations. NGO and utility to be responsible.

NGO will be the overall coordinator and facilitator of the implementation of the proposed activities.

The duration of the intervention implementation is expected to be two years (2004–06).

11.4 Expected benefits

The proposed intervention is expected to achieve the following:

*   Creation of opportunities for interaction and partnership between SWEs, utilities, and customers (households) for mutual benefit.
*   Provision of good quality water to households in the low-income settlement to safeguard the heath and well-being of the community.
*   Reduction of water charges by vendors to acceptable and affordable levels in view of closer location of utility kiosks in the settlement and hence reduced travel distance by vendors.
*   Mitigate against the health hazards (strains on chest and ribs due to pushing the carts long distances) that affecting pushcart vendors.
*   Reduce queuing time (as a result of increased water quantity and pressure) for consumers, especially women and street water vendors, when filling up at the utility kiosk.
*   Help more vendors to enter the water vending market (as a result of availability of good quality water source at kiosk) and thus create livelihood/employment for them.
*   Provide increased customer base and revenue for the City Water Services as a result of water sales at the kiosks.
*   Offer employment opportunities for existing SWEs to operate and maintain kiosks as agents under contractual agreement with City Water Service.
*   Create opportunities for SWEs to enhance and strengthen their water supply knowledge, entrepreneurial knowledge, experience, and management skills especially where the SWEs are given the opportunity to operate and maintain the kiosks on a commercial basis.

- Successful implementation of the pilot intervention would be replicated in other informal settlements in the City.

11.5 Conclusion

In the final analysis, the proposed interventions for Phase 2 will benefit consumers, SWEs and utilities (DAWASA, City Water Services and the Municipalities).

References and Bibliography

Boyd, Graham (2001) *An overview of Private Sector Participation in the Dar es Salaam Water and Sewerage Authority (DAWASA). A Report for WaterAid-Tanzania.* WaterAid-Tanzania, Dar es Salaam.

CEEST (1998) *Dar es Salaam Water Demand: An end-use perspective.* Centre for Energy, Environment, Science and Technology (CEEST Foundation), Dar es Salaam.

CIUP (2003) *Local Infrastructure Standards and Cost.* Community Infrastructure Upgrading Program (CIUP) for Dar es Salaam, May 2003, Dar es Salaam.

Dar es Salaam City (1999) *Strategic Urban Development Planning Framework,* Draft for the City of Dar es Salaam, Stakeholders' Edition, Dar es Salaam.

Gibb Eastern Africa (2002) *Review of Performance of Urban Water and Sewerage Authorities.* Gibb Eastern Africa.

GoT (2001) *EWURA Act. No 11, 2001.* Energy and Water Utility Regulatory Authority (EWURA), Dar es Salaam, Tanzania.

GoT (2001) *Dar es Salaam Water and Sewerage Authority Act (amended in 2001).* Dar es Salaam Water and Sewerage Authority (DAWASA), Dar es Salaam, Tanzania.

GoT (1999) *Water Laws (Miscellaneous Amendments) Act (1999).* Government of Tanzania, Dar es Salaam, Tanzania.

HBS (2002) *Household Budget Survey 2000/01.* Final Report, National Bureau of Statistics Tanzania, Dar es Salaam, July 2002.

Kjellen, Marianne (2003) *From Public pipes to Private Hands: Water Provisioning in Dar es Salaam Tanzania.* Stockholms Universitet (unpublished licentiate thesis).

Kyessi, Alphonce G. (2002) *Community Participation in Urban Infrastructure Provision. Servicing Informal Settlements in Dar es Salaam.* SPRING Research Series 33, University of Dortmund, Germany.

Mato, R.R.A.M. (2003) 'Towards sustainable groundwater management in Dar es Salaam City', *Journal of Building and Land Development.* University of Dar es Salaam, Tanzania, December 2003.

Ministry of Industry and Trade (2003) *SME Development Policy*, Ministry of Industry and Trade, Dar es Salaam, April 2003.

MoLHSD (2000) *National Human Settlements Development Policy.* Ministry of Lands and Human Settlements Development, Dar es Salaam, January 2000.

MoWLD (2002) *National Water Policy.* Ministry of Water and Livestock Development, Dar es Salaam, July 2002.

MoWLD, Water Aid, EASTC and NBS (2002) *Water and Sanitation in Tanzania: Poverty Monitoring for the sector using national surveys.* Ministry of Water and Livestock Development, WaterAid - Tanzania, Eastern Africa Statistical Training Centre and National Bureau of Statistics, Dar er Salaam. www.wateraid.org.uk/in_depth/country_programmes/tanzania/1396.asp

National Bureau of Statistics Tanzania (2002) *National Population Census.* Government of Tanzania, Dar es Salaam.

Water Utilities Partnership (2001) *Water and Sanitation for all. A Practitioners Companion.* Water Utilities Partnership, http://web.mit.edu/urbanupgrading/waterandsanitation/home.html.

WEDC (2002a) *Better access to water in informal urban settlements though support to water-providing enterprises.* Inception Report, WEDC, Loughborough University, December 2002.

WEDC (2002b) *Better access to water in informal urban settlements though support to water-providing enterprises.* Project Planning (Nairobi) Workshop Report, WEDC, Loughborough University, August 2002.

WEDC (2003) *Better access to water in informal urban settlements though support to water-providing enterprises.* Work Plan, WEDC, Loughborough University, March 2003.

World Bank Report (2003a) *Dar es Salaam Water Supply and Sanitation Project.* World Bank, Washington, USA.

World Bank (2003b) *Project Appraisal Document, World Bank Report Number 25249 – TA,* World Bank, Washington, USA. www-wds.worldbank.org/servlet/WDS_IBank_Servlet?pcont=details&eid=000 090341_20030508103932

WSP (1999) *Small Scale Independent Providers of Water and Sanitation to the Urban poor: A case study of Dar es Salaam.* UNDP-World Bank Water and Sanitation Program Washington, USA.

Appendices

Appendix 1

A1.1. Study Methodology

In order to get a comparative and more in-depth understanding of the livelihood strategies of vendors in the city, the study carried out intensive in-depth interviews with at least four SWEs operating in different parts of the city and serving different market segments (in addition to those in Sandali Ward). In particular the interviews with the SWEs focused on business opportunities which are related to the supply chains, how individuals react to opportunities in the supply chain, and what constrains or encourages them to take up opportunities and avoid threats.

The study conducted interviews with SWEs operating in the following market segments: low-income residents of informal settlements with no piped water; low-income residents of informal settlements with (inconvenient or costly) access to standpipes or other piped supply; small business users within the informal settlement; low-income people in formal settlements and better-off residents (see Table A1.1, below).

A1.2. Development of key research questions and techniques

Research methodologies and techniques and key research questions were developed on the basis of questionnaire guidelines given in the Project Planning Workshop Report (Nairobi, July 2000). The key methodologies used were PRA, focus group discussions and in-depth interviews.

The following questionnaires were developed to suit the research objectives:

1. SWEs   -   In-depth interviews/ Focus group discussions
2. Consumer   -   In-depth interviews/Focus group discussions
3. Utilities   -   In-depth interviews
4. NGOs and academics -   SWEs interviews

Table A1.1. List of settlements selected for study of SWEs and interviews conducted

Name of settlement (ward)	Type of market	Group of consumers	Group of SWEs available	No. of consumer FGDs conducted	No. of SWE FGDs conducted	IDIs conducted (consumers)	IDIs conducted (SWEs)
Sandali	Low-income residents of settlement with inconvenient or costly access to standpipes or other piped supply	Women Men Students Micro-enterprises Poorest people as defined by the community Bachelors with jobs	Street water vendors Private boreholes Community-managed boreholes Resellers of utility water	Women: 1 Men: 1 Primary school students: 1 Micro-enterprises: 1 Poorest as defined by the community: 1 **Total: 5**	3	20	6
Yombo Vituka	Low-income residents of settlement where no piped water connection exists	Women Men Students Micro-enterprises Bachelors with jobs	Street vendors Private boreholes Community-managed boreholes	-	1	-	1
Mtoni	Small business users within informal settlement	Women Men Students Micro-enterprises Bachelors with jobs	Street water vendors Owners of private boreholes Community- managed borehole Community-managed kiosk Resellers of utility water and resellers of utility water	-	1	-	2

Note:
IDI: In-depth Interview, FGD:-Focus Group Discussion

(Table A1.1. continued on next page)

Appendices

Appendices

Table A1.1. List of settlements selected for study of SWEs and interviews conducted *(continued)*

Name of settlement (ward)	Type of market	Group of consumers	Group of SWEs available	No. of consumer FGDs conducted	No. of SWE FGDs conducted	IDIs conducted (consumers)	IDIs conducted (SWEs)
Azimio	Low-income people living in formal settlement	Women Men Students Micro-enterprises Bachelors with jobs	Street water vendors Owners of private boreholes Community- managed borehole Community- managed kiosk Resellers of utility water and resellers of utility water	-	-		1
Kurasini	Better-off residents out of informal settlement but with unreliable connection	Women Men Students Micro-enterprises Bachelors with jobs Tankers/resellers Individuals connected from private boreholes industries	Private boreholes Community- managed street vendors				1
Buguruni (Ilala Municipality)	Low-income residents with inconvenient piped supply	Women Men Students Micro-enterprises Bachelors Tankers/resellers Individuals connected to boreholes Industries	Owner of private borehole and wholesale transporter using three water bowsers				1

To ease understanding of the questionnaires by both the interviewer and respondents the research team translated the questionnaires from English into Swahili.

A1.3.　Participatory Research Appraisal (PRA)

PRA methods were used to involve the community in gathering baseline information which links water access, water enterprise and poverty in Sandali Ward. This participatory method provides a way of sharing information between researchers and a cross-section of people in community, which more formal methods do not easily allow. The community mapping method involved the steps described below. The process began and ended with local community representatives, and each step depended on the information obtained in a previous step.

The process began with a meeting of invited sub-ward representatives familiar with the historical and socio-economic developments of the wards, and they identified the history, community issues and problems. The community representatives were made to take leadership in providing the information, including data on existing water supply infrastructure, services and management in their respective sub-wards.

Based on the information obtained in the first meeting, a second meeting attended by three to five members from each sub-ward representing elderly men/women leaders associated with the history of the settlement, small enterprises, households (male and female house owners/tenants), young men and women, street water vendors, private borehole owners, representatives of communities managing community boreholes, household resellers of utility water and people with disabilities was organized. This was to obtain an in-depth understanding of the historical and socio-economic information on community conditions, assets and problems including information on diseases common in the settlement and the links between water access, water enterprises and poverty.

A1.4.　Community mapping

All PRA members participated in community mapping. One study team member helped the group to prepare a map of the settlement and analyse data from the meeting and incorporate it into the map. They also framed additional data-gathering efforts in the field, identified and located on the map appropriate infrastructure and services, (water supply facilities, access roads, health facilities, schools, places of worship etc.), administrative local area boundaries, and other geographic features and information.

The team carried out field surveys to confirm all this information. A community map was prepared for the study.

Appendices

By designing and leading the mapping process, the community representatives were better positioned to ensure that the map accurately reflected community needs. Community leadership in the settlement was also made aware of the mapping process, which enables the community to use the resulting map for future advocacy, organizing purposes, and activities that may result from the research findings.

Problem listing and ranking

PRA members including men, women, old people, young people, street water vendors, borehole owners and owners of informal small business were asked to list and rank the problems in the study settlement (Sandali) in order to enable the participants and the study team to understand the community infrastructure and social services, issues and problems, needs and priorities, and to get relevant and representative data to help frame the data-gathering efforts.

Wealth ranking

Wealth ranking was used to establish the economic status of the members of the community. The group members classified members of the community into high, medium and poor as the distinct economic classes in the settlement.

Venn Diagram

A Venn diagram was used to identify and establish relationships between the community in the settlement and its community organisations.

Community history

Apart from other participants, two elders were invited by the research team to provide the history of the community.

Together with pre-testing, PRA methods provided the grounds for the research team to correct and restructure the questionnaires.

A1.5. Focus group discussions (FGDs)

Focus group discussions for water consumers and small water enterprises were held in Sandali, and for small water enterprises outside Sandali.

Five FGDs for consumers and three FGDs for SWEs were held for Sandali, and two for SWEs outside Sandali.

Essentially, the focus group discussions were in-depth guided discussions among several individuals ranging from 8 to 12 consumers or SWEs led by a female facilitator from the study team. The focus groups were used to answer specific questions and to explore the issues and problems.

The FGDs for consumers were meant to collect attitudes of consumers to SWEs. Thus the FGDs helped to obtain the experiences and perceptions of the group and cross-check information given by individual consumers concerning water supply aspects such as availability of supply, service options, technology, price and quality, etc.

The FGDs for SWEs were meant to explore and confirm important issues on SWEs' constraints, experiences, work practices, and opportunities and to help develop proposals for improvement.

Thus the FGDs for SWEs provided information on the constraints, experiences, work practices and opportunities of the SWEs as a group and cross-checked that initial in-depth interviews with individual SWEs were representative.

Conducting FGD meeting
The meetings were arranged in advance via invitations issued by the research team. The meetings took place indoors in the conference/meeting rooms of offices of the ward executive officer or the street (sub-ward) chairman and lasted two to three hours. The participants were given food after the meetings as an incentive. The turnout was satisfactory and the number of participating members ranged between 8 and 12.

A1.6.   Moderating FGDs
The objective of the research was explained to each group at the start of the meetings. During the discussions, the facilitator ensured that everyone in the group had a chance to speak and she endeavoured to move and control the discussions in a way that would not influence and affect the results of the group discussion by tactically minimizing any focus group emotional outbursts, ganging up on one person, irrelevant tangents and domineering personalities.

Documenting
Written notes of the FGDs were taken by two study team members during the discussions. The facilitator was not required to take notes.

A1.7.   Debriefing
The facilitator debriefed with the study team immediately after each group discussion and any specific observations about the group were recorded for reference.

A1.8.   In-depth interviews (IDIs)

The study team members conducted in-depth interviews with individual SWEs and consumers representing various customer segments in order to (a) get an in-depth understanding of the way in which water vending fits into the livelihood strategies of vendors and (b) to get an in-depth understanding of the attitudes of consumers to SWEs.

Six in-depth interviews (IDIs) with SWEs in Sandali and with four SWEs operating in different parts of the city and serving different market segments were conducted.

A1.9.   Conducting interviews

The in-depth interviews were arranged and conducted by the four study team members with the co-operation and support of the local street chairmen. There were no prior advance letters or information sent to those interviewed. The SWE premises were located with the help of local street chairmen in each sub-ward. The consumers were picked from different locations of the study settlements to at least represent a sufficiently fair and wide geographical representation of each sub-ward and the customer segment.

Each interview lasted about two hours maximum and was conducted in a location convenient to each respondent. The respondent was provided with a soft drink as an incentive. Before beginning the interview, the respondents were informed of the objectives of the research and that the information they would provide would remain confidential.

The interviews helped to: provide a history of water vending and consumer attitudes from respondents who had lived in the settlements for a long time; highlight individual versus group concerns; reveal that experiences and perceptions on water supply services may vary from person to person; provide a fast overview of the community in the settlements and its needs and concerns.

Unlike the FGDs, the in-depth interviews were easier to administer in that it was easier to speak to one person and keep his/her attention than to address a group and there was also a chance to follow-up on questions and probe for more details.

A1.10. Observations

The observation method was used by the research team to gather information that was intentionally or unintentionally not reported by the community members interviewed.

The observations made by research staff during the field research activities suggest that the local government and political leaders in the settlement as well as the respondents interviewed were cooperative, enthusiastic, talked eagerly with the research staff, and emphasized that they would be happy to see their ideas and comments being transformed into workable interventions for improving the water supply services in the settlement. All along, the research team had to explain the reasons for gathering information to ensure that the respondents clearly understood the objective of the research.

Appendices

Appendix 2

Terms of Reference for Researcher in Dar es Salaam, Tanzania

A2.1 Background

WaterAid is an international NGO active in the water sector, and with presence in a number of countries including Tanzania. In Tanzania, WaterAid has rural programmes in Dodoma, Tabora/Singida and Kiteto, and an urban programme in Dar es Salaam.

As part of its urban programmes, WaterAid is in partnership with the Water, Engineering and Development Centre (WEDC), Loughborough University, who are undertaking a research project entitled *'Better access to water in informal urban settlements through support to small water enterprises (SWEs)'*. The research is being funded by the UK Department for International Development (DFID). WEDC has a memorandum of understanding with WaterAid, through which WEDC is providing support and funding for implementation of the SWEs research project.

As part of the support, WEDC has prepared three key research documents which outline the research work to be undertaken in each of the four participating cities, Dar es Salaam being one of the cities. The three key research documents are:

- Project Planning (Nairobi) Workshop Report (dated August 2002)
- Inception Report (dated December, 2002)
- Work-plan (dated March 2003),

While the three documents provide important information on the research project, the Work-plan is a comprehensive document that provides details of the project purpose, conceptual framework, methodology, activities, and time-frame for the entire research project. The work-plan is therefore a key document for this project, particularly the implementation of Phase 1 in-country research work in Dar es Salaam which is the subject of these Terms of Reference.

WaterAid intends to contract Mr Linus Materu of EWAREMA Consult, to take up the role of Lead Researcher, to undertake and lead the in-country research in Dar es Salaam, and produce the specified research outputs. Mr Linus participated in the project planning workshop in Nairobi during July 2002, and has already studied both the Inception Report and the Work-plan.

Responsibilities of the Lead Researcher, (Mr Linus Materu)
The role of the lead researcher is to plan and undertake research work as stipulated in the project documents. The research purpose, scope, conceptual framework, methodology, activities, outputs and estimated timeframe are stipulated in the following key research documents:

- Project Planning (Nairobi) Workshop Report (dated August 2002)
- Inception Report (dated December, 2002)
- Work-plan (dated March 2003),

The lead researcher will work closely with the WaterAid team to plan and conduct research, analyse the results and prepare the reports for submission to WEDC. The lead researcher will work closely with the WaterAid Research Officer and the policy officer, both of who have social research skills. The Lead Researcher will maintain regular communication with WaterAid Programme Manager, Dar es Salaam, as well as with the Principal Researcher (Dr Cyrus Njiru) based at WEDC in the UK.

Research activities, expected outputs and timeframe
The Phase 1 research activities, expected outputs and time frame for undertaking various activities are summarized in Tables A2.1, A2.2 and A2.3 of the Workplan. It is expected that effort will be made to undertake all activities and produce all the anticipated outputs in a timely manner, given that Phase 1 of the project is running behind schedule. Rigorous work is expected in order to produce quality research outputs to international standards. All outputs will be word processed in English, and the outputs will be reviewed by an international review group, membership of which is detailed in the Workplan.

Time inputs, time schedule of work and deadlines
The following table provides an estimate of the time allocated for each group of activities. This may change depending on field conditions, but it is expected that the estimated overall time inputs will not be exceeded. If time inputs are considered insufficient, then the Programme Manager, WaterAid Dar and the Principal Researcher at WEDC will discuss and agree the way forward.

The total time inputs (Phase 1) for the Lead Researcher (Mr Linus Materu) will be in the order of 50 days in total.

In order to implement this Terms of Reference, a contract will be made and signed between the Lead Researcher and WaterAid, and a copy sent to WEDC.

As discussed during a meeting between Mr Linus Materu, Ms Wilhelmina Malima and Dr Cyrus Njiru at the WaterAid, Dar, offices on 2 September 2003, the start date for this assignment will be 15th September 2003.

Appendices

Appendix 3

Sources of Household Drinking Water and Distance to Sources

Table A3.1. Annual percentages of households with access to different sources of drinking water

	Dar es Salaam		Other Urban Areas		Rural areas		Mainland Tanzania	
Year	1991 / 1992	1200 / 2001	1991 / 1992	1200 / 2001	1991 / 1992	1200 / 2001	1991 / 1992	1200 / 2001
Piped Water	**93.0**	**85.7**	**72.7**	**75.6**	**24.5**	**28.3**	**35.9**	**39.3**
Private piped to house	22.1	13.7	20.3	15.1	1.1	0.8	5.2	3.8
Private piped outside house	52.6	19.1	22.7	17.0	3.3	2.1	9.2	5.5
Piped to neighbour	N/A	46.4	N/A	28.9	N/A	3.5	N/A	10.2
Piped in community	18.4	6.6	29.7	14.6	20.2	21.9	21.5	19.8
Other protected sources	**3.8**	**7.9**	**10.9**	**12.4**	**10.3**	**17.6**	**10.0**	**16.2**
Public well (protected)	3.5	4.7	10.5	7.5	9.4	13.3	9.2	11.8
Private well (protected)	0.4	3.2	0.4	4.2	0.7	1.4	0.7	2.0
Spring (protected)	0.0	0.0	0.0	0.7	0.2	2.9	0.2	2.4

Note:
Use of a neighbour's piped source was not included as an answer category in the 199/92.
'Other sources'

(Table A3.1. continued on next page)

Table A3.1. Annual percentages of households with access to different sources of drinking water *(continued)*

		Dar es Salaam		Other Urban Areas		Rural areas		Mainland Tanzania	
Year		1991 / 1992	1200 / 2001	1991 / 1992	1200 / 2001	1991 / 1992	1200 / 2001	1991 / 1992	1200 / 2001
Unprotected sources		1.8	3.6	10.1	11.2	63.9	53.2	52.1	43.6
Public well (unprotected)		1.7	2.2	5.5	5.1	26.5	21.2	21.9	17.5
Private well (unprotected)		0.1	1.0	0.8	1.2	2.6	3.8	2.2	3.2
Spring (unprotected)		0.0	0.2	0.4	2.0	11.6	12.4	9.2	10.0
River, dam, lake		0.0	0.1	3.4	3.0	23.2	15.8	18.8	12.8
Other sources		1.4	2.8	6.2	0.8	1.2	0.9	2.0	1.0
Total		100.0	100.0	100.0	100.0	100.0	100.0	100.0	100.0

Source: Household Budget Survey, 2000/01, National Bureau of statistics, Government of Tanzania.

Appendices

Table A3.2.	Annual percentages of household distances to drinking water in the dry season							
	Dar es Salaam		Other Urban Areas		Rural areas		Mainland Tanzania	
Year	1991 / 1992	1200 / 2001	1991 / 1992	1200 / 2001	1991 / 1992	1200 / 2001	1991 / 1992	1200 / 2001
Distribution of distance								
Less than 1 km	88.5	84.0	66.8	73.2	43.8	48.9	49.9	54.9
1 to 1.9	7.8	6.5	17.3	12.2	25.0	21.1	22.8	18.8
2 – 2.9	2.3	1.7	8.7	6.7	11.2	9.4	10.3	8.5
3 – 3.9	0.1	3.3	2.1	4.1	7.1	8.8	6.0	7.8
4 – 5.9	0.6	2.3	4.2	1.9	6.7	3.6	6.0	3.2
6+	0.6	2.2	0.9	1.9	6.1	8.2	5.0	6.9
Total	100.0	100.0	100.0	100.0	100.0	100.0	100.0	100.0
Mean	0.2	0.5	0.7	0.6	1.5	1.7	1.3	1.5

Note:
this table shows the distance as recorded by interviewers which were integers
('1 to 1.9' is '1' for example, source – Household Budget Survey, 2000/01, National Bureau of Statistics).

Table A3.3. Distribution of water source by poverty status						
	1991 / 1992			1200 / 2001		
Water supply	Very poor	Poor	Non-poor	Very poor	Poor	Non-poor
Piped	37.5	32.8	36.1	28.6	30.0	43.0
Other protected	13.3	11.3	9.0	16.9	18.1	15.7
Unprotected	47.8	54.4	52.6	54.4	50.9	40.2
Other	1.4	1.4	2.2	0.2	0.9	1.2
Total	100.0	100.0	100.0	100.0	100.0	100.0
Mean distance to drinking water (km)	1.2	1.2	1.3	1.7	1.6	1.4

Source: Household Budget Survey, 2000/01.

Appendix 4

People Contacted

People contacted during Phase 1 of the research:

Ministry of Water and Livestock Development (MoWLD)
Office of Principal Water Officer, Mr Kubena, Principal Water Engineer

Dar es Salaam Water and Sewerage Authority (DAWASA)
Mr B.N. Kasiga, Director of Technical Services, Dar es Salaam

City Water Services
Mr Mike O'Leary, Chief Executive Officer, Dar es Salaam

City Water Services – Temeke Area Office
Mr Francis, Area Manager

Dar es Salaam City Council
Ms Venus Kimei, Coordinator, Community Infrastructure Upgrading Programme (CIUP)

Ms Margareth Mazwile, Asst Coordinator (CIUP)

Temeke Municipality
Eng. Mosi, Municipal Water Engineer

Sandali Ward – (Temeke Municipality)
Mr A. Lekule, Ward Executive Officer

Mr W. Mwatandila, Sub-ward Chairman – Mamboleo A

Mr Salim Shamte, Sub-ward Secretary – Mamboleo A

Mr H. Minawandu, Sub-ward Chairman – Sandali

Mr H. Muki, Sub-ward Chairman – Mamboleo B

Mr A. Matimbwa, Sub-ward Chairman – Mpogo

Mr J. Mungi, Sub-ward Chairman – Mwembeladu

Yombo Vituka Ward – (Temeke Municipality)
Hon. Ngayonga, Ward Counsellor
Mr Kiwa Ninago, Ward Executive Officer
Mr Hassan Chobo, Sub-ward Chairman – Yombo Vituka

Mtoni Ward – (Temeke Municipality)
Mrs M. Marunda, Acting Ward Executive Officer

Kurasini Ward – Temeke Municipality
Hon. Kimati, Ward Counsellor

Azimio Ward Temeke Municipality
Ward Executive Officer

WaterAid, Dar es Salaam
Ms Wilhelmina Malima, Programme Manager, Dar es Salaam

Plan International (NGO)
Mr H. Mkoma, Programme Unit Manager, Dar es Salaam

Equal Opportunities Trust Fund (EOTF – NGO)
Mrs Fatma Riyami, Director of Finance and Administration, Dar es Salaam

University of Dar es Salaam
Prof. A. Mashauri, Professor – Water and Sanitation, Dar es Salaam

University College of Lands and Architectural Studies (UCLAS)
Dr S. Mgana, Head of Environmental Engineering Department, Dar es Salaam.

Appendix 5

Visit to Sandali and Yombo Vituka wards

Visit to Sandali Ward (28/10/2003)

People met:

Mr Lekule – Ward Executive (Interviewee)

Mr Salim Shamte – Secretary– Mamboleo A sub-ward.

Table A5.1. Population – Sandali Ward				
Sub-ward	No of Households	Men	Women	Total Population
Sandali	10,042	19,750	18,881	38,631
Mwembeladu	1,413	**2,649**	**2,568**	**5,217**
Mamboleo A	3,463	6,736	6,462	13,198
Mamboleo B (Close to Tazara)	888	1,854	1,719	3,573
				60,619

Source: Sandali ward office – Temeke Municipality.

Existing water supply situation

According to Mr Lekule, the water supply situation in the ward is as follows:

- There is no reliable piped supply from DAWASA network in the area.
- There is no network except in the Mwembeladu sub-ward.
- The residents rely on water supply from boreholes and shallow wells. The supply from the shallow wells is seasonal and unsafe due to presence of pit latrines in the area. Other sources include nearby river (Yombo River) and hand-dug wells in the river bed.
- Due to poverty many people fetch water from the polluted nearby Yombo River. The distance to this source is less than 1 kilometre. The Municipal Health

Authorities (staff) have been advocating:
- boiling water for drinking purposes; and
- use of 'water guard chemical' (chlorine) to disinfect vended water.
- Sandali ward is heavily prone to cholera outbreaks.
- Private water supply boreholes drilled by private drillers in the area were not subjected to water quality tests and regulation by the Ministry of Water & Livestock Development.
- Private boreholes and water vendors have improved the availability of supply in the ward especially from year 2000.

Existing sources/supply options in Sandali Ward
(List and number of sources is not exhaustive.)

- 1 borehole drilled by DAWASA
- 1 borehole in Sandali Sub-ward drilled by Tanzania Social Action Fund (TASAF)
- 2 boreholes in Mpogo Sub-ward drilled by Mr Farid and Wipers (Muslim charity organization/non-governmental organization)
- Shallow wells with handpumps constructed by Temeke Municipal Council
  - 1 in Mamboleo A
  - 1 in Mamboleo B
- Private boreholes
- Household resellers of DAWASA water (for households with a DAWASA water connection)

The above sources supply water to: communities, small informal businesses that consume water, and water vendors in the area.

- Generally the purchase price of water at source is TSh20-30 per 20-litre jerrycan. The same amount is sold by vendors at Th100–150 and may rise to TSh200 during water supply shortages.

Existing problems

- There is no network in the ward except a small one in Mwembeladu and Sandali Sub-wards. The piped supply is very inadequate; supply is intermittent and available for only a few hours in a day.
- Water supplied from some private boreholes is of questionable quality. Such boreholes are located in the close vicinity of pit latrines.
- One private borehole was temporarily closed by municipal health authorities on

court instruction pending adherence to water treatment requirements prescribed by the municipal health staff.

- The whole area is a squatter area; part of the area is earmarked for upgrading under Community Infrastructure Upgrading Project (CIUP).
- Frequent power supply interruptions affect continuity of supply from the boreholes equipped with electric driven pumps and increases the cost of water supply supplied.

Observations from discussions and in the field

- People living in the area are generally poor. The houses (permanent/ semi permanent wattle and daub housing) are congested and haphazardly arranged.
- Private and Community managed boreholes are the main sources of water in the area. Supply from private boreholes is more reliable because some of them are equipped with stand by electric generators.
- Community managed boreholes were financed by DAWASA, Municipality or Religious institutions and handed over to the communities to own, operate and maintain.
- Community boreholes are managed by a water committee.[5]
- The map for the ward (hand drawn) is available at the ward office.
- There is no control by municipal authorities etc. over price charged by water vendors.
- Control by municipal authorities is on the quality of vended water especially at the private borehole sources. The control is often not continuous. It is exercised more during periods of cholera outbreaks.
- Construction of shallow wells and boreholes close to pit latrines is discouraged by municipal health workers.
- During water supply shortages often caused by power supply interruptions, vendors travel to Buguruni over about 2 km distance to fetch piped water.
- There are problems in the management and accountability of funds collected by water committees (for community managed boreholes). Banking of collected revenue is not regularly done. Normally they are required to bank the revenue twice a week.
- Community water attendants are paid monthly wages. The water committees are usually given sitting allowances (TSh5,000/per sitting).

Observed livelihood activities

1. Petty trading:
   - sale of charcoal
   - sale of food
   - sale of cold juice and water

   Men's activities:
   - sale of second hand clothes
   - sale of vegetables
   - small shops and groceries

2. Informal labour at low levels

   Men's activities:
   - shoemaking and repair
   - carpentry
   - tailoring
   - car repair
   - welding
   - water vending

   Women's activities:
   - sewing
   - embroidery
   - mat making
   - tailoring
   - selling cooked food
   - local brewing

Visit to Yombo Vituka Ward in Temeke (28/10/03)

People met:

Mr Kiwa Ninago – Ward Executive Officer (Interviewee)

Mr Ngayonga – Counsellor

Table A5.2. Population – Yombo Vituka Ward in Temeke				
Sub-ward	No of Households	Men	Women	Total Population
B. Mwinyi	2,449	5,165	4,945	10,110
Kilakala	3,729	7,504	6.960	14,464
Vituka	2,721	5,757	5,742	11,499
Sigara	1,726	4,057	4,213	8,280
Machimbo	3,627	7,608	7,820	15,428
Total	**14,252**	**30,101**	**29,680**	**59,781**

Source: Yombo Vituka Ward Office – Temeke Municipality.

According to Mr Kiwa:

- About 99 per cent of the people in the area rely on boreholes and private shallow wells as the supply sources. They also use surface sources in valleys.
- There is no utility (DAWASA) distribution system in the area.
- The number of shallow wells was 97 as at 2002 (it has increased since then).
- The nine existing boreholes were financed by: Urban Sector Rehabilitation Project (three boreholes), and TASAF and others (six boreholes).
- Water vendors collect water from the sources and deliver it to households using pushcarts.
- Most people also go to the sources to collect water.
- Purchase price of water at source is TSh10–30 per 20-litre bucket at community-managed boreholes and goes up to TSh50 per bucket at one of the private boreholes. Many people do not prefer collecting water from the private boreholes because of the higher prices.
- Sale price by vendors ranges between TSh100–150 per bucket.
- Municipal health workers provide chlorine to street (sub-ward) chairmen (Wenyeviti wa mitaa) who in turn distribute the chemicals to the people in the community with instructions on how to treat water using chlorine.

- Water from most of boreholes generally has salty taste.
- Unlike in the past, cholera cases are on the increase.
- The price for selling water is determined by the suppliers.

---

5. According to the water policy, a Water Committee should consist of 8 members: A Chairperson, Secretary, Treasurer and five other members. At least 5 members of the committee should be women.

Appendix 6

Inventory of Boreholes in Mamboleo A, Mamboleo B and Mpogo sub-wards

Table A6.1. Inventory of Boreholes in Mamboleo A Sub-ward

1.1. Boreholes driven by electricity (table 1 of 3)

Name of borehole owner	Community borehole	Mr Ngemera	Mr Osmond Haule	Mr Ali Rashidi	Mr Juma Mkombo	Mr Masud Mtumwa	Mr Salum Ramadhani Lumala
Depth of borehole (meters)	46		60	70		25	
Yield of borehole (m³/hr)	1.0	5.0		1.0	20	4.0	2.0
Project cost (TSh)			Cost of pump TSh 350,000			Cost of borehole = TSh 400,000 Pump = TSh 200,000	
Monthly operating cost (TSh)							
Monthly electricity consumption (kWh)	37–40 kWh						

(Table A6.1. continued on next page)

Table A6.1. Inventory of Boreholes in Mamboleo A Sub-ward

1.1. (continued) Boreholes driven by electricity (table 1 of 3)

Name of borehole owner	Community borehole	Mr Ngemera	Mr Osmond Haule	Mr Ali Rashidi	Mr Juma Mkombo	Mr Masud Mtumwa	Mr Salum Ramadhani Lumala
Monthly electricity bill (TSh/day)			50,000	80,000	50,000	15,000	60,000
Revenue from water sales per day (TSh/day)	4,000	1,500 –2,000	2,000	2,000	10,000-	1,000	3,000
Price per 20-litre bucket (TSh)	10	20	20	20	20	10	20
Taste of water	Slightly salty	Slightly salty	Slightly salty	Slightly salty	Slightly salty	Slightly salty	Slightly salty
Additional information / comments from respondent	Borehole constructed by DAWASA in 1977 Water committee available Pump not working for more than six months	Private borehole constructed in 1998 Pump Attendant paid TSh15,000 per month	Electricity bill is too high Usually disinfects water once in a month	Most of revenue is used for paying electricity bills Water sales are very low during rainy season (March–May)	Private borehole constructed in 2003 using private drillers	Facing competition from other borehole owners Given funds he would install pipe distribution system	System not working. Pump motor burnt out five months ago

Appendices

Appendices

Table A6.1. Inventory of Boreholes in Mamboleo A Sub-ward

1.2. Boreholes driven by electricity (*table 2 of 3*)

Name of borehole owner	Mr Waziri Shaban	Mr Abas Mustafa	Mr Claud John	Mr Raphael Watena	Masjid Rahman Mosque	Mr Kikkides Frederic	Mr Daudi
Depth of borehole (meters)	25	37		-	31	25	
Yield of borehole (m³/hr)	0.4	2.4		5.0			
Project cost (TSh)	TSh700,000 (2003 prices)						
Monthly operating cost (TSh)							
Monthly electricity consumption (kWh)				-			
Monthly electricity bill (TSh/day)	18,000	23,000		30,000	50,000	30,000	60,000

(Table A6.1. continued on next page)

Table A6.1. Inventory of Boreholes in Mamboleo A Sub-ward

1.2. (continued) **Boreholes driven by electricity** *(table 2 of 3)*

Revenue from water sales per day (TSh/day)	1,500	1,500-2,000		3,000	4,000	2,500	500
Price per 20-litre bucket (TSh)	20	20	20	20	20	20	20
Taste of water	Slightly salty	Slightly salty	Slightly salty	Not salty	Not salty	Not salty	Slightly salty
Additional information /comments from respondent	Cost of electricity consumes almost all the revenue from water sales	He plans to lay a pipe distribution system to consumers Borehole constructed in 2002	Pump motor burnt out a month ago	Borehole drilled in 2003	Cost of electricity is high Borehole drilled in 2002	Borehole drilled in 2002	

Appendices

Appendices

Table A6.1. Inventory of Boreholes in Mamboleo A Sub-ward

1.3. Boreholes driven by electricity (table 3 of 3)

	Masjid Simba Mbali (mosque)	Mr Mkandara	Masjid Lyaquin	Community borehole (Mzee Mamboleo)		
Name of borehole owner						
Depth of borehole (meters)		26				
Yield of borehole (m³/hr)	12.0	4.0				
Project cost (TSh)						
Monthly operating cost (TSh)						
Monthly electricity consumption (kWh)						
Monthly electricity bill (TSh/day)	22,000		5,000			

(Table A6.1. continued on next page)

Table A6.1. Inventory of Boreholes in Mamboleo A Sub-ward

1.3. (continued) Boreholes driven by electricity (table 3 of 3)

Revenue from water sales per day (TSh/ day)	500			
Price per 20-litre bucket (TSh)	20	5-10		
Taste of water	Slightly salty	Slightly salty	Slightly salty	
Additional information /comments from respondent	Cost of electricity is too high compared to running expenses	Cost of electricity consumes largest part of the revenue collected	Capacity of pump is much smaller than safe borehole yield Water is for mosque use only	New borehole not yet put into operation Financed by African Relief Committee of Kuwait

Appendices

Table A6.2. Sandali (Mamboleo B sub-ward)

2.1. Boreholes driven by electricity

	Edina Cezia	Mzee Malenda	Mohammed Mwipi (community)	Moris Muhagama	Wilfred Kamera
Name of borehole owner					
Depth of borehole (meters)	18	70	73	-	18
Yield of borehole (m³/hr)	-	5,000 lt/3hrs	-	8,000 lts/3hrs	
Project cost (TSh)	1,500,000	4,000,000	500–1,000 per day	2,000,000	Repair
Monthly operating cost (TSh)	Borehole cleaning 5,000–7,000			About TSh 75,000	Repair 70,000
Monthly electricity consumption (kWh)	92 unit/week 370/ month		Handpump	-	-
Monthly electricity bill (TSh/day)	10,000/week 40,000/month		-	-	50,000–70,000
Revenue from water sales per day (TSh/ day)	6,000–7,000	150–1,000 /per day	9–190	12,000–15,000	1,000–5,200 (dry season) 200–600 (rainy season)

(Table A6.2. continued on next page)

Table A6.2. Sandali (Mamboleo B sub-ward)

2.1. (continued) Boreholes driven by electricity

	20	20	10	20	20
Price per 20-litre bucket (TSh)					
Taste of water	Slightly salty	Slightly salty	Slightly salty	Not salty	Not salty
Additional information / comments from respondent	It is expensive to pay for TBS certificate	Funding provided by donors		The source is located in Kiwalani in Ilala District Water is piped to kiosk in Mamboleo B	Needs a loan to purchase new motor

Appendices

Table A6.3. Sandali (Mpogo sub-ward)

3.1. Boreholes driven by electricity

Name of borehole owner	Aziza Gevas	Mpogo Mosque	Abdallah Kumbunga
Depth of borehole (meters)	34.0	40	24
Yield of borehole (m³/hr)	-	4.0	
Project cost (TSh)			
Monthly operating cost (TSh)	Servicing of pump - 10,000 / 3 months	5,000,000 Borehole cleaning 45,000 Salaries 45,000 Security guard 45,000 Electricity 30,000	Donor funded-Dinan
Monthly electricity consumption (kWh)	90 units per week		
Monthly electricity bill (TSh/day)	40,000	48,000–60,000	10,000
Revenue from water sales per day (TSh/day)		4,000–10,000	500–2,000
Price per 20-litre bucket (TSh)	10	20	20
Taste of water	Slightly saline	Good water not saline	Slightly saline
Additional information /comments from respondent	Revenue collected is little compared to running costs especially electric power supply		Financial assistance is required to purchase storage tank

Table A6.4. Sandali (Mpogo sub-ward)

4.1. Shallow wells

Name of shallow well owner	Community-managed shallow well
Depth of well	
Project cost	
Monthly operation and maintenance cost	
Water sales (number of buckets) per day	
Price per 20-litre bucket	Provided free
Opinion on water quality	Salty water
Traditional wells	-
Additional comments	-

Note:

1. Cost of replacing defective pump/motor is unaffordable to many of the owners of private and community-managed boreholes.
2. The electricity bill, according to the borehole owners interviewed, consumes most of the revenue collected from water sales.
3. Water from boreholes is salty but the salt content is acceptable to the consumers.
4. Borehole data and pump specifications were not available from the borehole owners at the time of the study. The borehole yield data provided is based on the owners' information provided concerning time required to fill the installed storage tanks.
5. Although the objectives of the research were clearly explained to the private borehole owners interviewed, it would appear that they were a bit reluctant to discl☐ provided might☐ bers of buckets sold per day, price of a 20-litre-bucket of water and the total revenue collected per day.

Appendix 7

Priority sub-wards, population and proposed number of kiosks in Phase 1 – CIUP

	Table A7.1. Proposed number of kiosks in CIUP Phase 1						
No.	Project area	Male	Female	Total	Ha	Density	Proposed No. of kiosks
1	Manzese Uzuri	7.885	7.512	15.397	36	427	9
2	Kilimani	6.807	6.716	13.153	47	287	12
3	Madizini	8.245	7.908	16.153	39	414	9
4	Mnazi Mmoja	4.705	4.484	9.189	26	356	7
5	Muungano	2.948	2,967	5.915	16	370	4
6	Mvuleni	3.446	3.243	6.689	15	446	4
Sub-total Kinondoni Municipality		**34.036**	**32.830**	**66.866**	**179**	**374**	**45**
7	Mnyamani	8.625	8.611	17.236	48	357	12
8	Malapa	6.428	6.484	12.912	34	380	8
9	Madenge	6.279	6.335	12.614	32	394	8
10	Mtambani	10.170	10.277	20.447	53	386	13
Sub-total Ilala Municipality		**31.502**	**31.707**	**63.209**	**167**	**378**	**41**

(Table A7.1. continued on next page)

Table A7.1. Proposed number of kiosks in CIUP Phase 1 *(continued)*							
No.	Project area	Male	Female	Total	Ha	Density	Proposed No. of kiosks
11	Chang'ombe A	1.996	2.013	4.009	7	573	2
12	Chang'ombe B	2.361	2.507	4.868	15	325	2
13	Toroli	4.016	3.968	7.984	17	470	4
14	Sandali	5.884	5.829	11.713	35	335	9
15	Mpogo	1.825	1.799	3.624	15	242	4
16	Mwembeladu	2.610	2.596	5.206	18	289	5
Sub-total Temeke Municipality		**18.692**	**18.712**	**37.404**	**107**	**350**	**26**
Grand total Phase 1[†]		**84.230**	**83.249**	**167.479**	**453**	**370**	**112**

[†] Phase 2 will involve installation of 138 kiosks in the City Water Distribution area.

Source: City Water Services, 2004.

143

End notes

Chapter 4

1. Thus SWEs comprise one category of micro-enterprises under the informal sector. In addition to filling a long-term water supply gap left by the utilities in the low-income settlements, SWEs provide employ-ment. According to the government policy for Small and Medium Enterprises, (SMEs) (Ministry of Industry and Trade, 2003), micro, small and medium-sized enterprises play a crucial role in employment creation and income generation. Out of 700,000 new entrants into the labour force annually, about 660,000 (94 per cent) join the unemployed or underemployed reserve and end up in the SME sector, and especially in the informal sector, generating their own livelihoods. Given that situation and the fact that Tanzania is characterized by low rate of capital formation, SWEs as a sub-component of SMEs need to be supported. Micro-enterprises employ up to four people, mostly family members.

2. Based on discussions held with City Water Services and a review of the World Bank Appraisal report, 250 kiosks are expected to deliver water to about 250,000 people. The 40 DAWASA community water supply projects are expected to deliver water to about 100,000 people (i.e. 2,500 people per project).

3. The National Human Settlements Development Policy (MoLHSD, 2000) estimates that unplanned areas accommodate about 70-75 per cent of the population of Dar es Salaam.

Chapter 8

4. Cost data obtained from SWEs' (borehole owners) focus group discussions.

Appendix 5

5. According to the water policy, a Water Committee should consist of 8 members: A Chairperson, Secretary, Treasurer and five other members. At least 5 members of the committee should be women.